He's Got Potential

He's Got Potential

A Field Guide to Shy Guys, Bad Boys, Intellectuals, Cheaters, and Everything in Between

Dr. Belisa Vranich
and Ariane Marder

John Wiley & Sons, Inc.

Published by John Wiley & Sons, Inc., Hoboken, New Jersey
Published simultaneously in Canada

Design by Forty-five Degrees Design LLC

For general information about our other products and services, please contact our Customer Care Department within the United States at (800) 762-2974, outside the United States at (317) 572-3993 or fax (317) 572-4002.

Wiley also publishes its books in a variety of electronic formats. Some content that appears in print may not be available in electronic books. For more information about Wiley products, visit our Web site at www.wiley.com.

Library of Congress Cataloging-in-Publication Data:

Lozano-Vranich, Belisa, date.
He's got potential: a field guide to shy guys, bad boys, intellectuals, cheaters, and everything in between/Belisa Vranich.
p. cm.
Includes index.
ISBN 978-0-470-26701-1 (pbk.)
1. Mate selection. 2. Man-woman relationships. 3. Women—Psychology. 4. Men—Psychology. I. Title.
HQ801.L696 2010
306.82—dc22

2009015965

Printed in the United States of America

10 9 8 7 6 5 4 3 2

Contents

1 Prince Charming Potential (PCP)

Ninety-four percent of women between the ages of eighteen and forty-five start thinking about how to change a man within the first four minutes of a date. A man would *never* say about a woman he just went out with, "She's got potential." It's almost a comical notion: two men are sitting at a bar, and one says to the other, "So, man, how was your date yesterday?" The other nods and replies, "Yeah, this one, she's got potential."

They each take a swig of beer. "If I can get her to swivel less on her golf swing," the second man continues, "she could break forty. And I'm sure that leg curls would take care of that bit of cellulite on the back of her thighs. She snorts when she laughs, but I can probably get used to that. Yep, this could be the ticket."

The first man slaps his friend on the back and says, "Good luck, man. You are more of an optimist than I, my friend. Remember that babe last year? I thought she was almost perfect. I thought I could change her. There were just a few little things that drove me nuts: that friggin' little dog of hers that she'd bring everywhere, that vegetarian kick she was on, and then the last straw—a Mets fan." Sigh. "But good luck, my friend."

Never. It never happens.

You, on the other hand, have said it a hundred times, and you've thought it twice as much. You are excited when you say, "Whew, baby, now this one, this one has some po-ten-tial!" Just a few tweaks, you think—whiten the teeth, throw out that dorky shirt he wears every third date, zap the propensity to quote *Superbad* or *Top Gun* at every possible moment—and he's golden.

Are you kidding? You become exasperated when you put together Ikea furniture or fix the glitch in the garbage disposal. Now you have a man who is hardwired to remember every Robert De Niro or Russell Crowe line ever uttered, and you think you are going to change him?

Regardless of your pathetic failure rate with past fix-it projects, somewhere inside you there is a voice saying, "Go for it. It'll be easy!" Are you high, girl? You have a better chance of birthing triplets at age fifty than slipping that gnarly shirt off the hanger and into the garbage without him noticing.

Rarely will a woman report, after a first date, that the guy is perfect exactly the way he is. No man is perfect. It's just that some have Prince Charming potential (PCP).

We polled friends, family, patients, and strangers to find out the most popular reasons women label men as guys with potential rather than as ideal. It's because he does or is the following:

- Bites his nails
- Watches sports too much
- Is not romantic enough
- Surrounds himself with immature friends
- Is messy
- Watches only dude movies
- Has terrible table manners
- Has funny tics
- Displays bad hygiene
- Has a bad sense of humor
- Doesn't get along with his family
- Doesn't get along with your family
- Is a people pleaser to an extreme
- Is a little chunky
- Looks at other women
- Has a very narrow food range
- Drives like a maniac
- Is terrible to take to parties
- Is jealous
- Is stingy
- Is moody
- Works too much
- Works too little

- Is always weighing in on how you look
- Is too controlling
- Hogs the bed
- Is too hairy
- Won't try new things

Women love to commiserate with one another about these things. Think about it: your friend tells you that her new boyfriend has an annoying habit of leaving dirty Q-Tips on her sink, and you can hardly wait until she's finished to tell her about your ex's dirty little habit of putting his toothbrush facedown on any surface in the bathroom. You never did get over his nose hairs, his mispronunciation of a particular word, the way he danced, or the fact that he didn't dance at all.

You both laugh. Then the conversation usually turns to how you failed to change him. You tried everything: cajoling, humor, bribery. Maybe you stumbled along, seething and nagging about the dirty toothbrush, until he slipped up with an indiscretion or a lie, and only then did you break off the relationship.

Perhaps the conversation turns to how the toothbrush guy also made you laugh all the time, was there for you through a crisis, or got your brother a job. You learned to rinse off the toothbrush and put it in the holder yourself because you realized that in the scheme of things, it was worth it.

There is a third, distant, possibility: that he actually learned to stop leaving the toothbrush around. There is a chance that something you said or did got through to him, whether it was a positive incentive (sex) or blackmail (no sex). Of course, this is the most desired outcome, because it seems to affirm that he really loves you. It's why women will gloat over successes in changing their boyfriends but linger over failures as if they were as personally meaningful as SAT scores.

Exactly *how* one managed to change a boyfriend is an essential part of this conversation. Tactics (usually subversive ones) are shared and analyzed. Women pride themselves on spotting PCP and on how they made their man change. Persistence, creativity, and the three Bs—bargaining, bribery, and blackmail—are the most common feminine fixer-upper tools. Women use them without any shame, and that is what blows men away: women will change men (or try to) without batting an eyelash, and then rehash the whole thing over salad with a friend.

Blame Music

For every feisty Pink song, every girl-powered TLC song, and, of course, Gloria Gaynor's "I Will Survive," there are hundreds of ditties playing in elevators, supermarkets, and gyms all around the country that are whispering the same message in your ear: love will conquer all. Male singers croon, "Without you, I am nothing." These messages are—surprise!—hogwash.

Whether you are divorced or holding out for a one and only, chances are that you want a man who will be a good gym partner, a vacation mate, your financial and intellectual equal, and someone who dreams as you do of bigger and better. Women now, more than ever, see that they have the choice not to marry or to stay single after a divorce. They are exploring all of the twenty-first-century options, which include coparenting and cohabitation as well as other alternative situations.

It turns out that marriage is not always such a great thing for women, and this is not a recent finding. In 1972 sociologist Jessie Bernard reported in her book *The Future of Marriage* that fulfilled single women lived longer than their disappointed married sisters. Men, on the other hand, needed to be married to live longer than their unmarried counterparts, regardless of their happiness.

Blame Hollywood

Nearly every "chick flick" out there, culminating with *The 40-Year-Old Virgin*, is about a guy with a heart of gold who has undergone a change in order to get the girl. At other times it's the woman who has to step up her game, whether it's learning to break-dance (*Step Up*) or trading in her poodle skirt for a pair of high-waisted spandex pants (*Grease*), all to show the guy that underneath it all, she is the one that he wants. She thinks, "You may not be attracted to a woman like me, you may be embarrassed or think we have nothing in common, but *I* will change your mind." Maybe the change she encourages is showing him that his soft side, the little boy inside him, is safe with her. Whether the man is Baron von Trapp, Rocky, or Jason Bourne, she can melt his icy heart. It's worth it; he has PCP.

It's hard to find a major motion picture that features a female lead who is content to be single. Almost every plot includes a romantic story line, preferably one that culminates in a big wedding. It's such an important device in feature films that the quality of the male partner seems to take the backseat. All he has to do is show up. *Sex and the City* was practically one long commercial for a wedding, and for what? So Carrie could marry the guy who had been stringing her along for years and then left her at the altar? In *Knocked Up*, Alison sidelines her successful career to mate with an unemployed pothead. In *Bridget Jones's Diary*, the heroine chases down a man in the street—in her underwear, in the snow. It didn't matter that he had just read her diary and started a fistfight at a dinner party.

In real life, you probably would recognize that being completely unreliable, unapologetically unemployed, or disrespectful of your privacy are significant, highly detrimental qualities in a boyfriend. If you're now thinking, "But I could change Mr. Big,

Ben Stone, or Mark Darcy!", it's important that you read through to the end of this book.

What Is Your Prince Charming Perspective?

You meet a man who is exactly what you've been looking for (pick one): tall, rich, funny, outdoorsy, family-oriented, wild in the bedroom, fanatical about workouts, and good to his mom and his sisters. Furthermore (pick another), he hates sports, loves shopping, likes to cook, actually does laundry, and is crazy about having in-laws. You have gone off the deep end thinking about how this tall, laundry-doing man will chat with your dad as he whips up some of his famous Bolognese.

He needs some tweaking, you say, but they all do. You know that he's not going to be perfect—who is? So how do you regard your new friend, who has so many good things going for him that all he needs is a little fine-tuning? Does he become your project? Is it your moral imperative as a girlfriend to help him out? Or will you try to make adjustments in successive approximations, hoping for a compromise? If you've ever had a boyfriend accuse you of being controlling, or if you've ever referred to him as a "diamond in the rough," a "fixer-upper," or a guy with "tons of potential," this is you. Don't worry; we are here to help.

Women who like to work on partners who have PCP fall into one of the three following groups. Which one sounds familiar to you?

- *The Civilizer:* All men need a little bit of refinement. The basics are there. He just needs someone to help him grow up. It takes a bit of time and a whole lot of patience, but the result is that you have a decent man who is grateful that you helped him to grow, and he might even chuckle with you over what a savage he was.

Subtext: You'll help him to grow. All it takes is a little TLC. The trouble is that you'll sound like more like a nagging mom than a girlfriend.

- *The Leveler:* You weigh the good qualities against the bad to see if the good ones prevail. For example, he's kind to you and your family, and he cleans up after himself; so what if he needs some more time to figure out what he wants to do with his life? You'll help him by being supportive and by introducing him to new ideas and the right people.

  Subtext: It's a give-and-take. You're not perfect, either. Being in a relationship means that you bring out the best in each other. The drawback here is that complementary traits never perfectly mirror each other; it's rarely a 50–50 percent situation.

- *The Sculptor:* You look at every man as a lump of moldable clay. Like an artist seeing the painting on an empty canvas, you view him as your masterpiece in progress. To be with you, he has to change. Whatever method (force, ultimatums, or guilt) you have to employ to make it happen, you will.

  Subtext: You love the challenge of a project. Within minutes of meeting someone, you start making lists of the things you'd like to improve. The problem is, when will you ever be happy?

These three descriptions have the same ingredients in common: your love will make him see the light; he'll weigh the wins and losses and come up with the conclusion that he needs to give up ___________, grow up and stop ___________, forget about ___________, or come to terms with the fact that your love is worth so much more than ___________.

Real Stories

"I grew up with the idea that everyone has faults. You took the good with the bad and then tried to minimize or extinguish the bad. For me, the bad was something I homed in on and tried to break down."

"To me it was just about adjustments and compromises that you make when you are with someone else, like sharing. Whenever you do something with anyone else, you always have to adjust—think of a roommate or a new tennis partner. I figured that if I was amenable to changing some things, he should be, too."

"I was about the project. Give me a messed-up guy, and all I would want to do is fix things around him. I'd start with his surroundings, then manage his life. He became my project. He needed me but hated me because he needed me. If I left, he would come crashing down again—I thought."

The Beginning

How did you get to this place? Experience and conversations with women have convinced us that it usually begins this way: After one date, or three or four, you think that he's quirky, but you know that you can smooth out some of his eccentricities. Perhaps he is normal and you are just waiting for some wacky thing to catch you off guard. Sometimes he has just hung around long enough to catch you on an off night when you happen to be a bit more open-minded. After a little wine and some good kissing, you figure that you can get over his one flaw—whether it's that he is a tiny bit condescending and protective or is actually proud of the fact that he has worn the same sneakers since 1998.

He needs a few adjustments, but he seems to be totally into your suggestions. You definitely think he has PCP.

At least, it *seemed* that he was keen on what you were saying. When you hinted that he needed to work on his self-esteem because he underestimated himself, he smiled—in agreement, you thought. You were more or less putting the bait out there, saying, "You could strive for so much more, you could be my prince." He heard you, and he smiled, which is universally understood as a positive sign—right?

Here's the catch. From his perspective, he only heard you softly say something about how great he was. He was hungry, and you looked really good. Whatever you said didn't require a reply (or so he thought), so he just smiled. You seemed happy enough with that.

Fast-forward a few more dates. You're still talking about his self-esteem problem (as you have termed it), and he's still smiling all the way back to your place. Everything is going fine, and he seems to really like you. So you decide to push, just a little bit harder, toward whatever it is you think would help him the most: therapy, a new job, or confronting his demeaning boss. You raise this issue. Once again, he only smiles. Not this time, you think, and you push again. This time you want a verbal response.

Here's where things can get sticky. The poor guy doesn't even know that he's been chosen for your makeover project. He just might not want to participate. Perhaps he's happy with the way things are, or maybe he doesn't want to date a life coach. At this point, you should drop it, but you won't. You've already decided, regardless of the odds, that you will make this guy over, even if it takes the whole year (or several). Besides, you've already invested *x* number of hours dating him, which doesn't include the time you spent getting ready for dates and pondering over what he should do in life in order to really showcase the PCP that you know he has.

Then confusion sets in. The relationship seems to be going well. He enjoys the things you like to do. He solicits your opinions; he is thoughtful and inquisitive. It seems as if he really likes you. Now, because he seems so into you, you start to wonder, shouldn't he want to change? Shouldn't he want to become someone you'll like even more, who can make you very happy? Does this sound familiar? Change the venue or the issue at hand. Does it ring a bell yet?

At this juncture, you must consider the obstacles between your man and his potential. You know that he has PCP, so there may be all sorts of reasons for his flaws. Some may affect you more than others. Does he drop out of sight because he's a pilot or because he just "forgets" to call? Is he moody because he hates his job? Does he wear that ugly shirt that he dubs "lucky" because he won the lottery wearing it? Most obstacles are removable, but *how* is another, bigger question.

You keep working on him. The longer you date, the more straightforward your suggestions become. It should come as no surprise that this often provokes a knee-jerk emotional response. For example, you've been dating for a few weeks, you've slept together a few times, everything is great, and you suggest being exclusive. The guy thinks, "I worked hard to get to be a ladies' man, and she wants me to be monogamous." Maybe he cancels dates to work late and is MIA on Sundays prepping for the upcoming week. You ask him to lighten up, to remember that life is short. He thinks, "My family encouraged me to be diligent, and now you're asking me to work less." You pull one way, he pulls the other, and the tug of war is on. He is thinking about getting promoted and job security and you are thinking of the priceless quality of time spent together.

The Game of Tug-of-War

The ball is back in your court. You've suggested something, he has resisted, and now you need to decide what to do. The big question is, how will you react when he does something that he knows you specifically want him not to do? For example, you've asked him to drive more carefully, but he's still doing eighty miles an hour past the elementary school. You've told him not to invite his friends over all the time, but they've been eating pizza on your couch for three days straight. Are you going to be able to keep your cool?

It can be endlessly frustrating to have the same conversation over and over—for both parties. It's possible that he's just forgetful and that as soon as you ask him to slow down, he apologizes and complies. Then again, he may give you the finger. If you ask him nicely to get his friends out of the house, it might jog his memory. If you reprimand him in front of his buddies, he's unlikely to be sympathetic to your request. Remember, you catch more flies with honey than with vinegar.

Still, no matter how nice you are, this situation is ripe for conflict. Maybe he shuts down and just doesn't want to hear your advice anymore (that he would be better off if he stopped biting his nails, getting too drunk, or dressing like a high school nerd circa 1987—of course he would be).

Here is where you have made your first mistake: you have assumed that he will be grateful that you believe in him. After all, he has PCP, and your intentions are so obviously right-minded. In fact, the more change you create, the more indebted he will be. Not only will you get the man of your dreams, he'll even thank you for it. This will bring the two of you closer and closer and closer—in your dreams.

I Don't Really Want to Change Him, I Just Want to Tweak Him a Little

You want the guy you're dating to just stop wearing one particular shirt or just stop telling one particular joke. There's always going to be one loose thread begging to be pulled. For most women, that thread is like a beacon. It's always there, in the corner of your eye. You tug gently at it, and you play with it when you're bored.

It might be an oversized leather jacket of his that you don't like, or maybe it's the story he always tells that gets on your nerves. He can certainly stop telling the one about "the blonde," but his sense of humor is going to remain the same. In a few weeks, someone will have sent him an utterly unfunny e-mail that he's now repeating at cocktail parties, and you'll be longing for the old lousy joke.

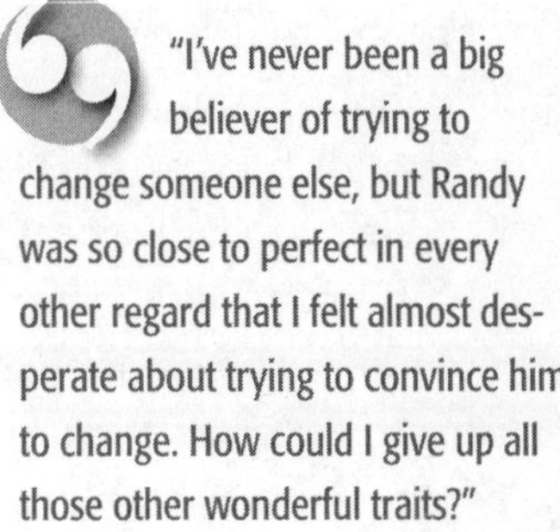

"I've never been a big believer of trying to change someone else, but Randy was so close to perfect in every other regard that I felt almost desperate about trying to convince him to change. How could I give up all those other wonderful traits?"

Why Are Women Like This?

There's a lot of unconscious thought behind your work on a man. Women tend to become invested in a relationship more quickly than men do, which means that women are willing to devote more energy to it. Being supportive is often an important component of the way that women show love. There are many other reasons that women gravitate toward men they want to change, that they are so lured by guys with PCP.

For many women, the desire to fix up a boyfriend comes from the same place as affection. It seems natural that because you like him, you want good things for him and expect him to want good things for you, too. You look at your man and think, "Since I care about you, I want you to be the best that you can be. The standards I set for you are determined by love. I want you to aspire to things in the same way I do. If I didn't like you, I wouldn't care about what you achieve in life."

A relationship is also a partnership, and as in any partnership, it's hard to keep everything equitable. You should certainly lend an ear if your man wants to unload and talk about his tough day at work. It's your job as a partner to help him feel better. You probably look at your boyfriend and conclude, "If we are going to be a team, then I have to encourage you, and you have to encourage me. That is what teams do."

Since relationships are joint ventures, many women, especially ambitious women, evaluate them the same way. For these high-powered women, their men have to fit with their vision for the future, and they're willing to help their fellow become that future if they believe that he has potential. Perhaps you gaze at your guy and say to yourself, "I have big dreams, so you have to step up to fit in my dream. I want you to be more polished, more successful, more sophisticated. How are we going to be an 'it' couple if you are satisfied where you are?"

The best partnerships involve people who have different skills. To you, it totally makes sense to be with someone because you are uniquely qualified to improve on his individual flaws. It feels like two pieces of a jigsaw puzzle coming together. You may take a good long look at your man and think, "The thing you lack is the thing I am good at. You are like work for me, but I am comfortable with work."

Women who are looking for a real challenge go for broken men the way that cats go for catnip. These women think that they are acting altruistically, and these men make them feel safe. A guy quickly opens up and maybe even becomes dependent on his new girlfriend, at least for a time. Perhaps you can imagine yourself actually saying, "You are damaged but approachable. Initially, you are grateful that I would even pay attention to you. Then I start pushing you out of your damaged approachable comfort zone and you are not as psyched to be with me."

There are a million variations on this basic theme. Flawed men strike deep chords in women. It is confusing because it seems like love, and it often is an essential part of love. However, it's important to recognize where your feelings are coming from—which nerve keeps being stimulated—especially if you always find yourself stuck in the same rut with boyfriends who just can't go the distance.

The Types of Women Who Love "Project Boyfriends"

Women who take on men who are "projects" are not all the same. Some do so consciously, others by habit. You either fit squarely into one of these categories or are a combination of two.

The Down Dater. Some women gravitate toward men who they know are somehow out of their league, and not in a good way. These men are often less attractive, smart, and accomplished than the women they go out with. If you haven't been one of these women, you've surely seen them: she has youth, beauty, and a great smile, and she's dating a man with thinning hair, a big gut, and a pocket protector. You might have thought, "He must have a lot of money," but that's not always the case. Some women are just suckers for an underdog because they can be cute, plucky, passionate, and willing to please. Does this sound like you?

"I love the underdog. I root for the losing team, the overlooked student, the character in the movies who is always coming up short. I want to be the woman in the movie in which the underdog wins, and he gets, well . . . me, of course."

The Rebel. There are women who just love to date men who they know are inappropriate. On some level, they enjoy it when their men break the rules. He's way older, he's way younger, or he doesn't speak English and that's the only language she speaks. Does this sound like you?

> "I love being defiant. It doesn't matter what I am defying. Ask me to do something, and I am automatically not going to do it. All you have to do is say to me, 'I don't think he is good for you! You are interested in *him*?' To which I will respond, 'Yeah, why not?' Then I will proceed to fall deeper in love with my physics professor, my questionable upstairs neighbor, or cellmate number 988-8098."

The Do-Gooder. Altruistic women who have gone through something bad—addiction, unemployment, depression—are deeply moved by someone struggling through the same set of circumstances. It's all so familiar, which can make it seem almost imperative that you help this man who is down on his luck—especially if your own struggles were difficult because you didn't have anyone to lean on. Does this sound like you?

> "Once I was in a bad place, and I needed someone to help me. Now that I've met him, I can do for him what I wish someone had done for me."

The Skeptic. A real cynic thinks that men are deeply, fundamentally flawed. Therefore, you need to find the most controllable jerk around; someone who will be putty in your hands. By the time you're finished with him, he won't be such a jerk anymore, but (you think) he will feel completely grateful and attached to you, and only you, forever and ever. Does this sound like you?

> "No guy is faithful. If I pick a real loser and fix him, he will stay with me. I can relax and totally be myself because he will be forever thankful."

The Frankendater. The most idealistic of all the women who are looking for a fixer-upper wants to start with a man who is pretty much a blank slate. He has to meet some basic standards, but you fully anticipate molding most things about him to suit your requirements: clothes, humor, sociability, friends, and so forth. He will be your greatest creation, your true Prince Charming. Does this sound like you?

> "I want to build the perfect boyfriend from scratch. All he needs are the basic qualities; I'll add the extras and make him over. At least he'll be predictable."

Sometimes the character flaws are there to stay, and you would rather bear them than take on every last thing. If he drinks only Budweiser and you love nothing but wine, you may be able to happily coexist under the same roof. Other shortcomings are not so easy, however. Take a look at the following list of imperfections and test your reaction. What can you live with and what can you help him to change? Your answers will be based on your own personal tolerance level.

- He has poor social skills: he's so shy that people think he's aloof.
- He has a bad sense of humor: he's crass, he's loud, he's immature.
- He is self-deprecating: he's so down on himself.
- He is moody and can be mean: you never know whether he's going to be nice to you.
- He is vain: it takes him longer to get dressed than it takes you.
- He is disorganized: he regularly misplaces his keys, wallet, phone, or passport.
- He is a flirt: you always find him talking to the pretty women. (That's how he met you!)

Prince Charming, I Know You're Out There

Face it: you are a princess even if the glass slipper doesn't fit your foot (Cinderella) or even if you don't sleep through the night (Snow White). For once you'd like to see a story about a princess who lines up all the guys in her village, makes them flex and cook her dinner, and then decides "I'm not settling down yet" and dates for another couple of years. That would be nice.

However, it's not just Disney that has contributed to the idea that there is a Prince Charming out there just for you. Every day, you hear someone refer to her partner as her "other half," her "soul mate," "the one," or "the lid to my pot."

Desire Disconnect

Tantalizing you like a carrot in front of a donkey is the notion of your very own Prince Charming, only you're not living in a fairy tale. Prince Charming is in your own mind. Who he is, what he does, what he likes, and how he behaves are all projections based on your lifetime of experience. The irony is that the experiences you've had don't necessarily add up to envisioning the most realistic of guys.

Women are always looking to change the men they date, but they seldom realize why that PCP is such tempting bait. Many don't carefully compare the list of traits they ideally want in their future mate with the list of things they actually need. In other words, be careful what you wish for. Your imaginary Mr. Right could easily become a huge disappointment in the flesh. You think you want a rich, worldly man, but in fact, you'll be lonely when he goes away on his frequent work trips. You think you want an athletic, healthy man, but then you'll be annoyed every weekend when he spends Sunday training and making protein shakes.

Unfortunately the disconnect between desires and necessity regarding a mate is pretty common. Sometimes women just refuse to let their fantasies die. Perhaps you're attracted to bad boys and their motorcycles, but when you really think about it, you realize that you want a man in the kitchen making romantic dinners. Since you are unlikely to find a bad boy who is also a homebody, you will need to revise what it is you are looking for and why. Women might want to be with someone like James Bond, who can be rough-and-tumble and then waltz them tenderly around a ballroom, but the chances are that they won't be able to find that guy.

It may seem as though you've already been struggling with this situation, dating guys who seem to have everything you want (or thought you wanted) but who invariably lack the characteristics you absolutely need. For example, you're unlikely to find someone who is just like you in terms of education and background but who is also going to be totally unpredictable. If you want someone who's financially stable, that same man is unlikely to want to quit his job and travel for a year. Some accountants do indeed rock climb, but you have to make sure that the desired and required qualities you're looking for in a man don't negate one another.

Define Your Search

Which type of prince are you looking for? At least, whom do you *think* you're looking for?

Type 1: "I want a guy who is my best friend. We will be partners in the adventure of life."

Example: We went to school for the same amount of time and are in the same industry. Sometimes we are even told that we look alike. We are in sync. We exercise and eat in similar ways. He feels like my intellectual equal. We even make a similar amount of money. He can read my mind, and I his.

Pros: Negotiating everyday life is easy. You know how he thinks by thinking about how you think.

Outcome: In your brain, similarity translates into relationship, and the more similar you are, the more he is relationship material. You are literally looking for you in male form.

Cons: Are you confusing the comfort of similarity with love? Will this end up feeling as if you are dating your evil twin?

Type 2: "I want a guy to save me. He will be my knight in shining armor and sweep me off my feet."

Example: He wants to take you away from your daily life and plop you into his. He pursues you eagerly and wants to incorporate you into his routine immediately. He loves to take you out to fancy dinners and give you gifts. He's romantic and traditional. He opens doors, pulls your chair out for you, and knows how to slow dance.

Pros: It's nice to be showered with attention. He makes you feel secure, desired, and beautiful.

Outcome: Every time you start dating someone new, you clear your calendar in case he calls. You evaluate each new relationship by how attentive the man is, and you would never think to pick up the phone (or a dinner check) yourself. You expect each date to blossom into a movielike series of romantic scenarios.

Cons: What is it about your life that makes you need to be taken care of so badly?

Type 3: "I want a guy who complements me, who is everything I am not."

Example: He's outgoing, social, and popular, whereas you are quiet and shy. You go to parties with his friends, and he does most of the talking, which is fine, because he's charming, funny, and smart (qualities you're not so sure about in yourself). When you take him to an occasional party with your friends, you can relax, knowing that he'll carry all the conversations. Sometimes you wonder if your friends like him more than they like you.

Pros: You can now experience the other side of life effortlessly. He holds your interest and satisfies your desire to be a different person.

Outcome: Every time you meet a man who strikes you as different from you in how he talks, dresses, or behaves, you think that he is your soul mate.

Cons: Could you work on the "missing" parts of yourself without a man?

Type 4: "I want a guy who is my better half, literally. He will make sure that I stay on the straight and narrow."

Example: Perhaps you have struggled with discipline or even drugs and alcohol. On your own, you tend to oversleep, miss meetings, and get too drunk at cocktail parties. Your boyfriend makes sure that you get up, reminds you about your appointments, and starts substituting water for alcohol if you become a little sloshy. He's like a safety net, ready to catch you if you slip up. He often scolds you for behaving badly, but you deserve it.

Pros: You can relax, knowing that your man will keep you in line. You feel supported and taken care of. It's kind of like having an assistant.

Outcome: You associate policing and discipline with love and affection. You find men attractive who, even if they hardly know you, will tell you what to do.

Cons: Are you looking to date the father you never had or the big brother you did?

Type 5: "I want a guy who provides a nice home and financial security. He'll be reliable and stable."

Example: You may never see him, but you know that he's working hard at being a doctor, a lawyer, or a businessman. He's occasionally stressed out, but you know that it's because he's working so hard, and you put your own concerns aside to take care of him (because he's the breadwinner). You often go out with him and his business associates and their wives. It's a conventional life.

Pros: You don't have to worry about money as long as you're with this guy.

Outcome: Every suitor is evaluated first by his bank account and second by his earning potential. You can't become interested in a guy who's not in a position to take financial responsibility for both of you.

Cons: Will you be able to live independently if he jets off with his secretary?

Type 6: "I want a guy to show off to my friends, family, and coworkers. He'll be gorgeous, smart, and accomplished."

Example: He's an international mergers and acquisitions negotiator who is always just getting off the plane (first class) from Zurich, Tokyo, or Buenos Aires. Nevertheless, he looks perfectly stylish and masculine. He tells great stories about negotiating peace deals in the Middle East. He looks like an underwear model. Everywhere you go, people want to know who he is.

Pros: It makes you feel awesome to show up with him wherever you go. Your friends and family are totally wowed that you could date someone who is so amazing on paper and in person.

Outcome: Each first date is like an interview. You evaluate potential mates by how impressed your high school best friend will be by his work experiences and his cheekbones. Even if you don't feel much chemistry brewing, if he's an Ivy League–educated, highly employed fashion plate, you'll go out with him again and again.

Cons: Is it fun to date someone else's supposed ideal?

What Is Your Prince Charming **Really** Like?

Tall, dark, and handsome may be a good place to start, but besides the obvious, what does this perfect specimen of a man have that you have been looking for? There are a million different characteristics that could seem paramount to you. If your family is your number one priority, your prince will have to fit right in with them. Your parents and your siblings have to approve of him, and he has to like them enough to want to spend time with them without putting up a huge fight.

Some women are intent on finding the best gene pool for their future babies. These women are saddled with an almost endless list of qualities to consider: intelligence, health, height, athleticism, emotional well-being, and so forth are all on the list of traits.

What traits make a man a Prince Charming in your eyes? Put a checkmark next to the ones in the following list that matter most to you:

Smart

Funny

Successful

Kind

Generous
Introspective
Extroverted
Athletic
Family-oriented
Good in bed
Ambitious
Good with children
Shy
Adoring
Good in the kitchen
Adventurous
Interesting
Well traveled
Well read
Stable

Is This a Female Problem?

We don't need to remind you that men and women approach the process of mating very differently. Men cast a wide net, and depending on confidence, alcohol, and peer pressure, they draw a porous line between the women who are good enough for the night and those who might be good enough for longer than that. The only real math they are doing is to evaluate what's on offer in any particular scenario: a potential girlfriend or a simple roll in the hay. Any woman who responds to their clichéd one-liner will fit into one or the other category—or will have a cute friend who is standing behind her.

Women, unlike their undiscerning counterparts, are choosy about whom they make eye contact with. Think about it: if you made eye contact and smiled at every guy at the bar, you'd be ambushed by all of them. Instead, your brain conducts a complex calculation that takes milliseconds, taking all of the variables into account. These variables are weighted and interchangeable: maybe you'll look at a guy who's too short, because he has great eyes and seems to be having a great time, or maybe you'll approach a guy who's dressed like a geek, because he's tall and stepped out of a Ferrari.

Women tend to be more realistic when it comes to dating. We talked earlier about women who date guys who are supposedly beneath them. You've probably known loser men who seem to get the best women. For some reason, they attract a lot of women and disdain dating anyone with any of their own flaws. They do this by finding women who want to fix them. Maybe these men stick around only until the nagging becomes really annoying, but in the meantime, they're satisfying their needs.

In addition, women are constantly getting feedback about themselves from girlfriends, magazines, television, and people on the street. Since how women look is generally considered so much more important than how men look, they're always asking their friends for advice: "Do you like these jeans on me? Should I cut my hair shorter?" Most guys couldn't care less if their jeans are good for their shape or if they use too much gel in their hair. Men's magazines, unlike women's magazines, are constantly telling their readers how hot and awesome they are; no wonder they go out ready to chat up any XX chromosome carrier in the vicinity.

Given these stacked odds, women are practically destined to be more flexible about who they like, because they're interested in having far fewer romantic partners. Men are wired in the other direction. They'll nod at everything you say if there is a chance of bedding you. They may never call you again, but that's another book. In the next chapter we'll explain in more detail how men's and women's brains work to encourage your fixer-upper instincts.

Finally, maybe you keep picking men to fix up because you have the notion that asking for more is being too picky. Maybe you don't think that you deserve someone who is already as fabulous as you are. Nevertheless, you either have a guy like this now or you keep picking this type and losing. That is why you are reading this book, isn't it?

Real Stories

"I would make a direct line for the most broken guy in the room. If he looked sad, confused, angry, or lonely, I was all over him. First I'd figure him out: let him talk and talk, ask questions, and become the world's best listener. The more information I got from him, the more I thought that our relationship was special. I knew things he had never told anyone."

"Jeff was cheap—not frugal, just cheap. He'd cut corners, try to get me to cut corners, try to take seconds for free, and bargain every chance he had. He was so cute and charming when he did it that it didn't bother me at first. Then one time I started thinking that he just didn't want to pay the extra couple of bucks for me, and I was livid. As far as I was concerned, if he tried to save money at other times, so be it, but why when he was with me? Wasn't I good enough?"

"Frank was frugal; he wouldn't spend a dime on himself. I'd look at his old towels and sheets and his worn-out clothes and want to fix them myself. Soon I was buying him things. It never came back around, though. The unspoken rule was that if I wanted something changed, anything from a new comforter for the bed to new soles on his shoes, I'd have to get it."

2 It's Not My Fault, It's My Brain!

If you've been wondering why you are such a sucker, consider that the problem is right behind your eyes. To a certain extent, the whole dance you're doing with Project Boyfriend was written in the gray matter of your brain tens of thousands of years ago. The steps may seem outdated, because they are. Your brain is doing the jitterbug, and everything else is crunking.

Unfortunately, you are even less likely to be able to change the way your brain processes information than you are to change your boyfriend. However, the point of this chapter is to show you how your perceptions are shaped and, to some extent, even predetermined by the big blob in your skull. If you can connect your reactions to your relationships to possible neurological events, you may be able to understand yourself and your situation better.

We mentioned in the previous chapter that women are more selective about sexual partners than men are. This is a biological phenomenon and not just a sociological one, and the selectivity doesn't include just biologically "perfect" men, it also includes imperfect men with potential. A woman's biological goal is to have a partner with whom to procreate but also with whom to have an emotional attachment. Thus, even though women are selective in choosing a mate with (real or perceived) access to material resources or social status, they are more flexible with the rest of their classification; that is, the rest is "fixable." The more accommodating a woman's definition of a satisfactory partner is, the greater are the chances of her procreating.

You think you've got chemistry with a man. The two of you click, and the love juice in your brain starts flowing. You feel crazy and high, and you just can't get enough of each other. The flood of hormones stewing in your brain blinds you to his flaws. He is adorable, fun, smart, and sexy. All of the potential problems you might have (or will probably recognize only in retrospect), like his video game addiction or his poor decision-making skills, are little bits of fluff floating on the wind of your passion.

Why do all of his quirks seem cute, and all of his oddities just details? One reason is well explained by Dr. Helen Fisher, a biological anthropologist who is an expert on the biology of love and attraction, in her description of the three stages of love: In the first stage you experience spikes of testosterone, norepinephrine, oxytocin, and vasopressin. Add a big dose of dopamine in the second stage, and you end up with the profile of someone who is a bit nuts and/or high.

Fast-forward into the future, to the third stage: you are in couple's therapy or bashing your head against the wall about issues that were there (clearly or with small red flags) from day one (or at least month one).

Why didn't you leave once the oxytocin wore off and those little bits of fluff became as irritating as fingernails on a blackboard? The next hormonal shift is not much fun, because the ecstasy-inducing love neurochemicals wane, and reality sets in. Now your dreamboat seems to be more of a fixer-upper, and this is when your brain starts to really screw you. Women are socialized and genetically wired to be nurturing (regardless of whether they are mothers), patient, empathetic, and ready to give the benefit of the doubt to others. These are admirable qualities. It's almost as if women have a positive gene in their makeup for making lemonade out of lemons: they see Lassie's fidelity in mangy mutts, they redefine old as "vintage," and were doing extreme makeovers long before they were ever done on television.

Furthermore, since women tend to invest more of their energy in a relationship, they are keener to work it out and less interested in cutting bait. You may find yourself frustrated at what seems like a man's unwillingness to put even the slightest bit of effort (from your point of view) into changing for the sake of your relationship. Research on women shows that getting along is intensely important to them, whereas for men it is less so. Competing is what they strive for. Apply this finding to a situation in which one person won't put his cup in the sink, and the other is waiting or hinting and hoping for him to learn. That's your relationship.

Perhaps you are now thinking that just explaining yourself better will help. Sorry—that's not going to happen.

Women are communicators, and you'll find yourself running into the concrete wall that is his inability to understand you, even when you speak really slowly and clearly. This is where the difference in

Face It

Studies on how well men read facial expressions report that they are far behind women. Women can read subtle facial expressions faster, and they need to see others' facial expressions in order to feel connected. It is not surprising that one study found that women felt nervous around men who were stone-faced.

neurochemicals comes into play. Estrogen makes you extremely talented at talking, reading someone's facial expressions and body language, and intuiting people's feelings. Testosterone, in contrast, shortchanges these very same brain pathways in men. Thus, you are left with the distinct impression that you are dating a lazy, unemotional dolt, yet you still can't find the front door.

This Is Your Brain on Love

You think about love and you think about your heart. The truth is not very romantic—it's much more about your brain: perception, calculation, and processing, part conscious and part unconscious.

1. Boy Meets Girl

When Joe first spotted Jane across the bar at his local pub, he knew two things: first, she wasn't a regular, and second, he wanted her to be. There was something about her that seemed to make her stand out from the crowd, something magnetic. Before he even realized it, he was standing behind her, inhaling her intoxicating smell. They had not even exchanged words yet.

We have shocking news for you. Men are more reactive to physical attractiveness than women are. This superficiality is not their fault; it's biology. Men look for a few key physical markers in their potential mates: facial symmetry, puffy lips, and clear skin. These traits signify not only attractiveness but also health and fertility. Now you understand the booming businesses of rhinoplasty and collagen. This sensitivity to the physical means that men are more likely than women to experience "love at first sight."

Within a few minutes, Joe was like a baby duck imprinting on its mother. Jane, meanwhile, had not even noticed him yet. He cleared his throat—no response. Finally he decided to try using words. "Can I buy you a drink?" he asked. Jane, engaged in conversation with two friends, cast him a sideways glance and without hesitation said, "No, thanks."

In this case, Joe was a little out of his league. Jane, a former dancer and model, was unimpressed with Joe's paunch and flannel shirt.

Joe thinks, "She is hot. I like her. I want to be with her."

Jane thinks, "No."

2. Girl Meets Boy

Joe recovered from the sting of rejection as he went back to his seat across the bar. He sipped his way through several whiskeys, which girded him for another attempt. This time, perhaps on drink three or four herself, Jane accepted Joe's offer of a drink. Joe sat down next to Jane, and almost immediately, the bartender, who had practically ignored Jane and her friends all night, was there to take their order. He said to Jane, "I didn't know you were a friend of Joe's! He's so impressive. To have been so successful at such a young age!"

Whoa, didn't that bartender just up the ante? According to neuropsychiatrist Louann Brizandine, author of *The Female Brain*, the fact that "our mental instincts haven't changed in millions of years may explain why women, worldwide, look for the same ideal qualities" in a mate—that is, "material resources and social status." In other words, if he seems like a good provider with a strong, supportive network, women are temporarily forgiving of the quirks and consider them possible to improve.

Jane has utterly forgotten Joe's paunch and flannel shirt. In fact, she may already be thinking things like "Wow, a little belly means he's not obsessed with diet and exercise. He's not vain!" or "To think, he has millions of dollars and wears a flannel shirt. I bet he's a salt-of-the-earth kind of guy." Joe hit on Jane because she was hot, but Jane welcomed Joe's overtures only when she knew he was successful. It's not the most profound of human exchanges, but it happens all the time—because of women's brains.

Brizendine and other scientists have explained that women are great compromisers when it comes to romantic partners. Since human babies are really work-intensive, and were especially so back when people were rubbing sticks together to make a fire outside the cave, women are attuned to finding a partner with the greatest number of available resources for potential offspring. The ability to control fertility with artificial devices has been around for only the last half-century of human history. Women are built to make the wisest long-term choices for reproduction; men, in contrast, don't have the same sense of responsibilities programmed into their brains.

Jane and Joe go out for a few weeks, and before she realizes it, she is in full-blown, "he is perfect" love. They see each other all the time, and she just can't get enough of him—all of him, from paunch

Desperately Seeking . . . Sperm?

According to *Science News*, the newest research on fidelity shows that women are unfaithful almost as much as men are; in fact, about 10 percent of children are not born to the man who the mother claims is the father. The newest research on monogamy brings up another factor. Any desperate housewife can tell you that even though women want a partner at home, they also continue seeking "good sperm" outside the home. Is your project guy the one you want to help you build a home? Do you want these two characteristics to merge in one man?

to flannel to any number of other distasteful traits that are presently masquerading as lovable quirks. Meanwhile, Joe is as happy as a pig in mud. He's dating the hottie from the bar who didn't even want to talk to him at first, and now they have sex at least three times a day.

Love is not something to be taken lightly, especially at the start of a relationship. During the first rip-your-clothes-off phase of love, according to Dr. Fisher, the lust is equivalent to drug addiction—specifically, amphetamine addiction, which is confirmed by actual brain scans. Hopeless romantics are both intrigued and saddened to learn that the crazy-in-love phase is neurologically about the same as being on speed.

The extreme pleasure of this phase is related to the sense of being wholly connected to another person. Psychologists call this feeling of losing yourself in another *merging*, and it resembles the feeling that an infant shares with its mother when they are connecting on a profound level. A vital part of an infant's development is "mirroring" the faces and expressions of the parents. In couples, the hyperattunement that two people experience to each other leads them to feel telepathically linked. When it's one-sided, it's similar to referential thinking, which can make you feel psychotic ("That song was telling me to call you"). When it's mutual, it creates a bond between two people that makes them feel something truly magical, even fated, about their meeting.

Add to this intoxicating feeling the dating reality that you two are still on your best behavior. Joe has been jogging in the mornings to impress Jane, and he rarely wears that flannel shirt because they're always going out to nice dinners that require a jacket and a tie. Jane doesn't really care about that stuff, anyway, because the seats in the first-class cabin to Paris are so comfortable and wide.

Jane thinks, "He's perfect."

Joe thinks, "She thinks I'm perfect! She's so cool."

3. Boy Is Not Perfect

A few months later, Joe and Jane have settled firmly into boyfriend-girlfriend status. They see each other a few times a week, check in almost daily, and are starting to shed their "best behavior." Jane finds herself scrutinizing Joe. She has come down from the clouds and is back in her own brain and skin again.

As the rush of passion slows, the female brain shifts gears into a more sustainable mode. Neuroscientists recognize this as a distinctly different set of processes than the crazy-in-love state; after all, humans would probably not have survived if they had spent their entire lives after puberty in passionate love. Who would have taken care of the babies, stored food for the winter, and kept the precious fire burning?

After the first rush, the human brain in a relationship starts to produce new hormones. In women, oxytocin starts to dominate the emotional landscape, whereas in men, vasopressin does. These two neurohormones work to achieve the same thing: a lasting relationship. Studies of other mammals have shown that just being around one's mate increases the vasopressin in male brains and the oxytocin in female brains. These surges lead to higher levels of dopamine, the brain's pleasure elixir, thereby cementing the positive reinforcement that is associated with your loved one. That two different substances elicit the same response in men and in women is the best evidence we have about how different the male and the female brain are in relationships.

Nevertheless, this hormonal orchestra is not as potent as the druglike haze of early days. At breakfast one day, Jane looks across the table and realizes that Joe is wearing that same old flannel shirt—for the third day in a row. Then there's Joe's weight. Jane is a former dancer and has battled eating disorders for most of her life. Joe is a former fraternity guy who loves pizza and beer.

Joe is also a little older than Jane, whose father died of a heart attack when she was only fourteen years old.

If these roles were reversed, a few things would change. Joe might say to Jane, "Hey, Jane, you should lose some weight and put on a new shirt." Maybe Joe would say, "Hey, Jane, this isn't working anymore. I'm out." In all likelihood, however, Joe would not even have approached Jane to begin with if she had been sporting a gut and a ratty shirt.

Jane thinks, "He's almost perfect—just a little nip here, a little touch-up there . . ."

Joe thinks, "Hey, wait a minute!"

4. Girl Starts Project

Consciously or unconsciously, Jane goes to work on Joe. She begins hinting to Joe that he needs a new shirt. Then, instead of cooking pasta for the third time in a week, she volunteers to make him a skinless chicken breast. When he comes home with another six-pack, she pouts, hoping that he'll pick up on her disapproval. She does everything she can, short of holding him down and ripping the shirt off his back and the beer out of his hand.

When he doesn't respond to her nagging, moping, and the age-old telepathy attempt, her frustration starts to mount. He, in turn, becomes angry. "You're not exactly one to talk," he says. "I don't get on your back for always losing your keys." That's true, Jane thinks, but this is different. "I want to help," she says. "I don't want anything to hold you back from the person you could be."

Whereas most men who have unearthed an undesirable quality in a woman might move on with no second thought about it, a woman's sense of devotion keeps her dedicated to the cause. Her forgiving nature allows her to see through the imperfections to the man underneath. She is optimistic that there is something to work toward, a relationship to be had; at the same time, she is forgiving of the little missteps in reaching that goal.

Jane thinks, "I will break him."

Joe thinks, "I will not be broken."

5. Girl Hates Herself for Hating Boy

Jane becomes annoyed with herself for harping on these things. She has moments where she thinks, "Maybe I'm being too hard on him." Then a few minutes later she changes her mind: "I'm just trying to help him. What does he think, that this is actually fun for me?" She vacillates between being angry at Joe and being angry at herself.

That starts the vicious cycle of blame. Jane can't figure out why Joe can't make a few simple changes without putting up a fight. She tries different kinds of threats to see what works. She's seen her parents work things out in fights, so she uses the same tactics they did. If you are a kindergarten teacher or a circus animal trainer, you use the tactics of positive and negative reinforcement. You pretty much just keep repeating your strategy, hoping that you'll eventually get the response you want.

Jane thinks, "What is wrong with him?"

Joe thinks, "Women are crazy."

6. Girl Decides She Definitely Hates Boy

Jane becomes very angry that Joe is "deciding" to ignore her or disrespect her, given all that she does for him. Men are wired to dig in their heels (or go into the ring), whereas women are wired to meet someone halfway. As we mentioned earlier, women's brains are programmed to get along (then add a heavy dose of being socialized to compromise), and men's brains are designed to compete (which is also enhanced by their socialization).

Ever since they were little boys, any opportunity to run farther, add or subtract faster, or beat an old video game score has ignited them. Once puberty hits, the competitive streak extends to the dating world. Since the beginning of time, male mammals have battled for mates, and recently scientists have found that rivalry affects how much sperm a man produces. Studies have shown that if a man suspects infidelity, his sperm count actually rises, in order to ward off the possibility of another man impregnating his partner. Thus, nature has devised a plan for you, or at least given you a framework through which to understand why he won't cave in to your "suggestions" or at least compromise.

Jane thinks, "I deserve better."

Joe thinks, "I'll have sex with every woman I can get my hands on."

7. Girl Puts Boy on the Scale

At this point, Jane starts to weigh the pros and cons of the relationship. "Sure, he is defiant when I ask him to change his shirt or mention that he eats too much red meat, but we have the most amazing sex, and he tells me that I'm the most beautiful woman he's ever seen." She starts to think that maybe it's not the end of the world if he's not an Adonis. He treats her well, brings her flowers unexpectedly, and is downright decent.

Research indicates that this may be just what Jane needs. A study conducted at the University of Texas and published in 2008 in *Evolutionary Psychology* ("Attractive Women Want It All") shows that women want four things from long-term relationships: economic resources, good looks, nascent parenting skills, and loyalty and devotion. The longer a woman has to wait to find the perfect mate, however, the more she'll begin to lower her expectations.

Jane may become annoyed by some of Joe's idiosyncrasies, but they alone might not be enough to send her running for the door. That's where ICK, or impossible character kink, enters the picture. ICK is a specific act that drives you crazy; it's the bad habit, the lazy twitch, or the tendency to do something obnoxious that makes you absolutely want to scream. It's possible that the ICK in question isn't significant enough to throw off the balance. If the basic qualities are there, then he still might be worth keeping.

Jane thinks, "Is he worth it?"

Joe thinks, "I wish I understood what the hell is going on here."

Maybe It's Just the Hormones

The above aren't everyone's scenarios; maybe you mutually fell in love the day you met, or maybe he was a blind date and you were well matched, point for point. What is consistent is the tendency of a woman to want to see her guy improve or change for her. Maybe the desire to change him comes from a nurturing stance, or maybe it comes from annoyance because he embarrasses her. Regardless, the goal is to keep the guy and fix the quirk.

Maybe your Joe is not a millionaire, but he does all right for himself and he is persistent. Jane (you) finally gives him a chance and finds that he is so attentive that she can't give him up.

Maybe you've taken a page out of *The Year of Yes* (a book by a woman who decided to say *yes*, for a year, to every man who asked her on a date); you've become tired of saying *no* to guys, so you decide that you'll just say *yes*. You are tired of hearing that you're too picky, and you are tired of jerks who seem to have it all together on paper.

"I see James as a grown man who has little-kid traits. He's obtuse and has his head in the clouds sometimes. For me, changing him is just about bringing those other parts of him up to speed. This feels natural to me, like something you'd do with a little kid: encourage good behavior and discourage bad behavior. I don't mean to treat him like a child, but I naturally want to encourage him to do more and be better. Is that wrong?"

Maybe the ICKs really come at you from left field once the man you're dating becomes comfortable and lets down his guard. You are sitting on the fence, wobbling between his obvious good traits and his obvious (at least to you) annoying ones.

The Neurological and Hormonal Reasons That Women Have a "He's Got Potential" Mind-Set (Or: ICKs Are Inevitable, So Why Don't Women Just Leave if They Drive Them Nuts?)

1. Women are givers. They are wired to be more forgiving and polite. Maybe women are more forgiving of the ICK even when it does bother them. Rather than fight against it, they hope that it will change on its own, or they try to make the situation more bearable. Seven forgiveness-related studies by Case Western Reserve University psychologist Julie Excline followed fourteen hundred students for seven years. Excline found that women are more empathetic, having been taught from childhood to put themselves in the shoes of others, whereas men tend to be more vengeful.
2. It's not only wiring, it's hormones. Whether you like it or not, many of your attitudes have to do with where you are in your monthly cycle. If you feel social, confident, flirty, or exhibitionist, it's probably about a week after your period has ended, when you are ovulating and most fertile. Are you less clear-headed or sensitive to strong smells? It's probably the week before your period. The drastic changes in progesterone and estrogen levels throughout the month can influence the way you think and feel in ways you don't even know. Research shows that you are more apt to like men with high testosterone on days seven through ten of your cycle. A week later, you might find yourself wondering why in the world you were so interested in Mr. Macho. A study

published by *New Scientist* found that on the days leading up to women's fertile time, they even become more susceptible to corny pickup lines.

3. The nose knows. You might think that you make rational decisions about whom you want to spend time with, but it actually all comes down to scent—the natural kind. Maybe you just like the smell of his sweat. Research has found that a chemical found in male sweat can heighten female arousal. A study done at the University of California at Berkeley by Claire Wyart and Noam Sobel in 2007 reported that androstadienone (a derivative of testosterone) caused women's cortisol levels to rise within fifteen minutes of sniffing it and to remain elevated for more than an hour. Similarly, a Rockefeller University study published in 2008 looked at male odor as a "social signal." When women ovulate (and can get pregnant), their response to androstadienone is strongest. In 2009 a Rice University study found that the female brain recognizes and encodes the scent of male sexual sweat. Male underarm sweat has been shown to improve women's moods and affect the secretion of their luteinizing hormone, which is normally involved in stimulating ovulation. The brain recognizes this chemosensory information, which can add to or detract from the senses of sight and hearing. Thus, if you are ovulating, his sweat supposedly smells good to you, so this could enable you to disregard his bitten-up nails or his squeaky voice.

4. You asked him if he'd change, and he said yes—well, sort of. So you see, it's not your fault after all. Dr. Daniel Amen, author of *Sex on the Brain*, cites a study that found that men, when faced with a pretty woman, make poor choices about math and money. Put the two of you together and it's no wonder that you're both puzzled about what you

were thinking when you met. The answer is nothing. You weren't thinking at all, you were dominated by hormones. His got in the way of logic ("No way am I getting rid of my favorite black high-top shoes!"), and yours made you pick a guy who was good for making babies but not for talking and problem solving the rest of the month.

5. You figured you'd take a fixer-upper this time. Maybe you picked him because you unconsciously thought that although he needed a little work, at least you'd get a guy who was psyched to be with you and not afraid to say it. Science knows how you feel. In a study published in 2008, the Association for Psychological Science found that "compared to females, males are more influenced by how physically attractive their potential dates are, but less affected by how attractive they themselves are, when deciding whom to date." Research supports this: couples in which the wife is better looking than the husband are more positive and supportive than other combinations. "The husband who's less physically attractive than his wife is getting something more than maybe he can expect to get," James McNulty, a researcher at the University of Tennessee, told LiveScience. "He's getting something better than he's providing at that level. So he's going to work hard to maintain that relationship." In the same interview, Dan Ariely, a professor of behavioral economics at MIT, adds, "Men are very sensitive to women's attractiveness. Women seem to be sensitive to men's height and salary." McNulty's study, published in the *Journal of Family Psychology*, says that wives are looking for supportive husbands.

"I figured I'd try dating Art, even though I was sort of out of his league, because I could fix him up. I wanted a guy who knew he was lucky to be with me."

The Happiness Gap

Betsey Stevenson and Justin Wolfers, economists at the University of Pennsylvania (and a couple), looked at the traditional happiness data and wrote about "the happiness gap" in the November 23, 2008, edition of the *Boston Globe*. Women now have a much longer to-do list than they once did (including helping their aging parents). They can't possibly get it all done, and many end up feeling as if they are somehow falling short.

"Are We Having More Fun Yet?", a study prepared for the Brookings Panel on Economic Activity in the fall of 2007, found an even starker pattern. Since the 1960s, men have gradually cut back on activities they find unpleasant. They now work less and relax more. During the same period, women have replaced housework with paid work—or, more often than not, have *added* paid work to housework—and, as a result, are spending almost as much time doing things they don't enjoy as they did in the past.

The *New York Times* reported in an article published on April 10, 2007, that forty years ago a typical woman spent about twenty-three hours per week in an activity she considered unpleasant—forty more minutes per week than a typical man spent. Today, with men working less, the gap has risen to ninety minutes.

It Wasn't the Man, It Was the Situation

A small earthquake hits while you are talking to Harry from the information technology department. You cling to each other for a few seconds; then, as the dust settles, you find him surprisingly cute. Where in the world did that come from? A little adrenaline rush and a small reminder of the fragility of life now have you thinking sexual thoughts. A landmark study found that men who crossed a wobbly bridge found the female examiners on the other side more attractive than men who didn't cross the bridge did. Studies on arousal have looked at how scary movies or even just working out at the gym can heighten a sense of attachment toward someone of the opposite sex who is near you.

Neuroscientists at the University of Pennsylvania found significant differences between the sexes in the way the brain reacts to psychological and performance-related stressors. Men responded with increased blood flow to the right prefrontal cortex, which is responsible for the "fight or flight" instinct, whereas women had increased blood flow to the limbic system, which is associated with a nurturing and friendly response.

He Can't Read Your Mind

Even if you think that you've pulled out all the stops in getting through to a man, the truth is that all the hints and suggestions you've been throwing his way may not be enough. It probably doesn't come as much of a surprise to you, but men are not as astute as women are at reading the emotional states of their significant others.

A 2008 study of married and unmarried couples conducted at the Hebrew University of Jerusalem found that women were more perceptive when they described their relationships but that both sexes were off the mark when they rated each other on issues like independence, abandonment, and sexuality. The men assumed that the women felt less independent, more afraid of abandonment, and less sexual than the women actually reported. This proves that communication about emotionally laden topics is essential.

Whatever bothers you doesn't get easier with time, either. The irksome traits that get under your skin now will only become more irritating with age. Research conducted at the University of Michigan revealed that people in long-term relationships tend to view each other more negatively as time goes by. Kira Birditt, a research fellow involved with the study, points out

(continued)

that negativity can stem from intimacy and be a sign of emotional closeness. (Remember the old adage "Familiarity breeds contempt"?)

Adversity Breeds Passion

Let's say, in our scenario, that Joe was offered a job across the country or that Jane's parents didn't like him. Maybe Joe's ex-girlfriend came back into his life. As in the case of Romeo and Juliet, there is nothing that will seal the deal more quickly than a little hardship in the relationship. Just tell two adolescents that they can't date, and see how fast they start climbing in and out of second-story windows to get to each other. Teenagers grow up, but this urge doesn't.

Predestined to Cheat?

According to a 2008 *Washington Post* article, scientists at the Karolinska Institute in Sweden found that two out of five men carry a gene that makes them less likely to settle down with one woman. The gene variant in question regulates vasopressin. Men who do not have the gene report not only that they feel less of a tug to stray outside of their relationship but also that they tend to be more emotionally available and loving. Current research is also finding that women are far less monogamous than was ever believed in the past.

Are Men More Forgiving, or Are Women More Demanding?

A study in Britain found that 80 percent of women reported being irritated by their husbands, whereas 60 percent of men had complaints about their wives. Being taken for granted ranked high on the women's list of complaints, followed by untidiness.

Q and A

Q I started dating a guy who was okay looking, and as I got to know him he became better looking to me. What is that called? Does it happen to men, too?

A Our poll of men and women found that as a woman starts to feel more connected to a man, he'll look more "adorable" to her. It's almost as if she loses perspective on what he looks like objectively. Seeing him as kind, even quirky and sensitive, will make her describe his looks with positive words, even when previously she might have thought of him as plain and dull. Men, in contrast, can find mean, cruel, and even dull women beautiful.

Q My boyfriend annoys me a lot, but when we have sex, I change my mind about breaking up with him. Somehow, that connection convinces me that I can change the things that bother me, and we start all over again.

A What happens to you makes perfect sense—maybe not to your thinking, logical brain, because let's face it, the habits that annoy you are not going to change. However, researchers at Wilkes University in Wilkes-Barre, Pennsylvania, have documented that good sex lowers blood pressure, increases the capacity of the immune system, decreases pain, and leads to a good night's sleep. Who wouldn't run back for more? Let's just hope that staying together makes more sense now, rather than that you are simply under his spell.

Beer Goggles?

More than 78 percent of the couples we studied met in social situations like parties and bars.

Beer goggles is the name for the phenomenon that occurs when you've had a few drinks and suddenly all the people who looked only semiattractive at first now look pretty good. In 2002, researchers at the University of St. Andrews and the University of Glasgow in Scotland took eighty college students and had half of them drink a "moderate" amount of alcohol: between one and four servings, depending on the person's sex and body weight. The other half, the control group, remained sober. Scientists showed each subject pictures of people of the opposite sex. In all cases, male and female alike, the experimental (tipsy) group rated each picture an average of 25 percent more attractive than the sober group did.

Here's what happens after each drink:

1. Alcohol stimulates the nucleus accumbens, the area of the brain that decides how attractive a person you are looking at is. An increase in perceived attractiveness seems to be directly proportional to the amount of alcohol consumed.
2. Factor in the observer's eyesight quality, the distance of the observer from the observed, and how brightly lit the area is, and you have what one group of scientists at the University of Manchester in England considered a mathematical formula for the beer-goggle effect.
3. You consider yourself an independent thinker, but you have two friends who think that Joe is kind of cute, and a third chimes in that he sort of looks like George Clooney's younger brother from one angle, so you find yourself considering him for a minute rather than standing firm with your knee-jerk reaction that he isn't your type. You value their opinions, so all of a sudden his worth goes up a few points. Add a few more mixed drinks (see above), and you find yourself kissing the pudgier version of George. Half an hour later, you are doing much more than just kissing. Oxytocin, the bonding chemical that mothers and babies and new couples feel, is whizzing around your body along with the tequila you were drinking. Fast-forward, and you are keeping a box of tampons under his bathroom sink and he is keeping a razor in your medicine cabinet.

3

Meeting His Representative

When you first met him, you couldn't believe that you had finally found someone who enjoyed going to plays—so what did it matter that he drank Dr. Pepper for breakfast or hadn't held a steady job in the last two years? For the first few months you were still just getting to know each other, so you were not even dating the real man; you were dating what's best thought of as his *representative*. That is, he was on his best behavior because he wanted to impress you and would do anything to woo you. Thus, in retrospect, it's quite possible that you did not overlook his idiosyncrasies; rather, he actually went out of his way to hide them from you until you were smitten with him.

Fast-forward, and you now find yourselves transitioning into the comfortable phase of the relationship. At this stage, the sheen of new love starts to fade, and the little things that you once thought were endearing start to annoy you. All of a sudden it really, really bothers you that he never puts a roll of toilet paper on the holder, that he sends text messages to others while he talks to you, that he has a "small" porn collection, that he sometimes chews tobacco, and that he dislikes your best friend.

Beware of EDE

Early dating effect (EDE): (1) the result of lust and attraction that is usually associated with the early stages of a relationship; (2) the combination of chemicals in your brain that leads you to minimize the flaws of the other person.

The Chase: Love and Game Theory

If you could only freeze him in time, that would be incredible: those moments that he leaned in and listened, referenced things you had talked about in the past, admired and remembered what you wore, and told you that you smelled good. This is the crux of the problem. You took into account those behaviors and noted them in the part of your brain that remembers things with excruciating detail. Then you really screwed yourself: you thought that this was his baseline, the starting point from which he could be changed. Were you ever wrong!

That period was like a job interview for a very, very motivated applicant. He was showing you the absolutely best side of himself. Unfortunately, this was not the baseline; it was the "this is as good as it gets" level of him, something you'd see only during the chase phase, while his brain was swimming in epinephrine and endorphins. The result is that he turned on the charm, used every trick in the book, and tried being cute, confident, sweet, and debonair. While he was courting you, his dating senses were on full alert, and he had plucked every errant hair and rehearsed every line before the mirror.

Once he got you—whatever that meant to him—he relaxed. Now you are both oozing hormones, cuddling, and feeling comfortable. You are probably even encouraging him, without realizing it, with your loving "I'll get that for you, honey, don't get up" kind of behavior. He then makes the fatal mistake of thinking that this extremely easygoing stage is where you are going to stay. You let things slide, easily moving from annoyed to laughing when he does his Joe Boxer dance; you might even start coming up with silly pet names for his eccentricities. Then the next phase—reality—sets in.

You Put Out the Bait; He Bit

Let's examine this next phase step by step:

1. You feel duped. You ask yourself if you are remembering those first weeks accurately. You might not realize it, but during that initial stage you put out the bait, and he bit. You aren't crazy. Women test men with the most complex questions and situations at the beginning of a relationship. Well, maybe *test* is not the right word; it's simply that women ask questions to gauge what they can expect. He's not on the same wavelength, however; he is, instead, looking for the right answer, the one-liner that will make you fall for him. While you are looking for information, he is giving you the answer that he thinks you want to hear.
2. Definitions are an issue. "Do you like to travel?" you ask. "Love it," he answers. The catch is that his definition of

travel is one trip a year to Disney World, whereas for you it's weekly bed-and-breakfasts and road trips to interesting corners upstate. When you want to go to Vermont, he digs in his heels because there is no Pirates of the Caribbean ride there. Didn't he say he liked traveling? Perhaps *traveling*, to him, requires hiking boots and a tent, but to you any place without window screens, air conditioning, and indoor plumbing reminds you of awful summer camps and scary bugs. When he says he loves exotic food, he means the spicy, unrecognizable innards that are considered delicacies in other countries—animals that you think would make good pets, not good appetizers. For you, *exotic* goes only as far as sushi or Thai food—that is, red meat, poultry, or fish that bears no resemblance to the living animal from which it came.

3. Women (and this is definitely a female fault) tend to magnify the significance of rather trivial things: "He went and got me some water; then I knew he'd be an attentive father for our future children!" "I was sick, and he offered to bring me soup; he's a perfect, sensitive life partner." Your wanting him to have the potential to be the perfect mate makes every detail meaningful, when in fact it's not. Before you give him a badge of honor for opening the car door, make sure that he's shown you *several* instances of being sensitive or kind, then stop yourself from making the jump to what this means for him as a fiancé, husband, father, or life partner until the second date.
4. If a man does the "right" thing, a woman will tell that story for months, even years, to her girlfriends. He apologized that his phone rang, he told the caller he was with the most beautiful woman in the world, and then he turned off the phone. He noticed that your napkin fell and, without hesitation,

got you a new one. He put his face near your hair and told you that it smelled incredible. He noticed that your panties matched your bra. Your remembering a detail, dwelling on it, and recounting it makes it much bigger and much more important than it should be.

5. As you are chattering or listening to him during phase one of meeting and being attracted, another misunderstanding arises from the fact that when he doesn't say *no*, you think it means *yes*. You explain why you don't eat veal—the way calves are raised is cruel, and the meat is not particularly healthy. He doesn't disagree, which gives you the sense that he must agree, at least halfway. The reality is that he's just learned to keep his mouth shut when he disagrees (at least at this point in the relationship, when he is trying to give you the impression that you are so right for each other). A man in chase mode will be on high alert to impress you in any way he can. He'll whiz through reams of information in his head: "chick flicks," sisters' advice, *Cosmo* cover headlines—to come up with the "right" answer. He's not being malicious; he just wants to provide the answer that will impress you, make you smile, and make you want to go to bed with him. Your goals, in a certain respect, are similar: you want to like him, and he wants to be liked. For what and for how long is where you differ.

What Was He Thinking?

He gave the "right" answer: the one that you wanted to hear but that was not really the truth. He was thinking that he was going to show you the best he could be, so that when you saw all his other wonderful qualities, you'd let the little annoying things slide. The problem is that you were doing almost the exact opposite: you were looking at his behavior at this moment as his baseline and coming to the conclusion that this was a diamond in the rough; you hadn't had a chance to work on him yet. These are two completely opposite frames of mind.

The Lust for Change

Wechsellust: (German) a yearning for change (*wechsel* = change; *lust* = desire); in this case, adjusting, maximizing, or extinguishing behaviors that are fantasized in another to create the perfect partner for oneself.

Then there is another scenario. What happens if he is lukewarm about you, yet somehow you've maneuvered a date with him? Is your lust for change the same? Somehow you've cornered a guy who you think is out of your league. Is your change fantasy different? Is the list shorter? Is there a list at all? The first thing you want to do is to make him realize what a catch you are, which is very different from the usual dynamic we have been dealing with here. Your radar is focused on what you can do to snare or entangle him, to make him aware of how perfect you are together.

Your Best Self Versus the Real You

Women also send their "representatives" to their first encounters. Women are often the fun-lovin' party girls who, once they become comfortable, want to turn to more "important" things. Then the guys don't get it. The number one complaint from men is, "Why doesn't she like to go out with me anymore?"

It's complicated, because convincing a man that you are his perfect mate should never be the dynamic. It leaves you in an unequal position in which you are hypervigilant about the things you might say or do that turn him off, and it leads you to constantly seek hints about what you can change to make him like, then love, you. If it goes awry, many women then waste time trying to convince him from afar of what he is missing. If he starts to somehow move along in the right direction, then women are constantly on alert in case he strays for another who is more his style from the start.

Time Reveals His ICK

In the last chapter we discussed *impossible character kink*, or ICK: the annoying habit that is simply the last straw for you. Maybe your boyfriend hid his ICK the first few months, or maybe it just didn't show up, for whatever reason.

Then maybe his ICK jumped out at you, and you didn't react. On your second date, he stared at the waitress as she walked away, but he brought his focus immediately and lovingly back to you. Right then and there, you could have said something. You might have nipped it in the bud. You didn't, though, because you didn't want to seem like a psycho.

Instead, you decided to play it cool, and you chose (that's right, *you chose*) to let it go. Maybe you even let him off the hook, telling yourself, "He's probably looking at the TV set," which was sort of in the same direction as the waitress as she walked away. Maybe you were overwhelmed by lust or alcohol, and your annoyance came and went in a flash.

Fast-forward to your twentieth date, four months later, and he does the same thing. This time, the initial passion has calmed, you're off the epinephrine sauce, and there's not one single television or distraction in the bar. He checks out the waitress again, and despite the fact that you chose to ignore this behavior before, you are now ready to leap across the table with your fork in your fist and scream, "Die, you jerk!"

Clearly, you are freaking out. Your brain is screaming, "I like this guy! I hate this guy! I could like love this guy! I want to kill this guy!" Like a car with a broken-down engine, you can feel the vapor hissing out of you. The "I like him" brain waves crash into your observations of how he clams up around your friends and picks at his teeth with his ATM card.

Keep in mind that not all ICKs are created equal. It would be great if you could just plop him on an ICK scale that would give you a quantitative measure of how likely this particular problem is to go away (or be chased away by you). A low ICK score would mean that you should enjoy him for the evening, the weekend, or maybe even the whole summer but that he has an expiration date as immutable as the one on a carton of milk. He'd come with a label you'd read as if you were looking for ingredients, calorie count, trans fat, or serving size.

Unfortunately, there's no ingredients label or warning tattoo from his last girlfriend, so you will have to do the assessment yourself. As you probably intuitively recognize, it's a lot easier to get your sweetie to wear socks than to ditch his lame friends. Maybe you buy him a few nice pairs of socks for Christmas. Maybe he loves them. Maybe he then becomes a guy who wears socks with sandals, and you hate that. What do you do then?

He Feeds Your Fantasy

"What's your type?" a friend asks you, and as you describe your ideal man, she goes through her mental Rolodex of single or almost-single male friends. You haven't really thought in depth about your description, however. You are imagining a Denzel Washington attitude with a bit of George Clooney, but what you describe is Jerry Seinfeld. Maybe you describe him as a guy with a confident walk.

Therein lies the problem: how does one define a confident walk? You have an image of the ideal man, but God knows how long you've had it. Is it the same guy you used to fantasize about when you were fifteen? Is he charismatic with an amazing smile, the type of guy who would take a bullet for you? The blind date you were sitting across from last Friday might have matched that description, but he still didn't make your heart go pitter-patter. Yet on you go, holding on to the same image of your "ideal" man, so you keep being disappointed.

Here's the predicament: at age twenty-five or thirty-five, you are really looking for other things, and your definition is outdated. Give it up! Certain qualities might have translated, in your adolescent brain, to "manly" things, but now in your adult life ten or twenty years later, a nice smile just means that he had a good orthodontist.

Sense of humor is the perfect example. It makes the top five qualities of 88 percent of women's descriptions of the perfect man, according to a Harris poll. Unfortunately, a man who thinks he's funny, or whose friends think is funny, is just a good stand-up comedian or likes telling jokes. Most guys who think they're funny like to perform for an audience, but it doesn't necessarily make for good conversation punctuated with laughter. What you really mean when you say he has a sense of humor is that he is light-hearted, laughs easily, finds your stories amusing, and will chuckle along with you at animal bloopers.

Your image of the ideal man can motivate you not to settle for less but to keep searching the earth for him. However, sometimes it will kick you in the behind. Watch out for the fantasies that have a high possibility of backfiring:

1. What are the clichéd qualities that you believe make a good man?
2. When and where did you first hear them?
3. When you look around, do you see them in reality?

The Wedding Fantasy

The ridiculous wedding fantasy is alive and well. It drains women of resources despite the fact that, knowing the statistics, the whole congregation should politely chuckle when "death do us part" is uttered. Does your relationship fairy tale culminate in a lavish wedding with envious friends looking on? How much do the tux he is wearing and the big rock on your finger counterbalance the issues you will have to deal with after the wedding? Is there really a rock big enough to quell your frustrations for the rest of your life?

Internet dating has forced people to examine what they want. Does he really have to be taller than five feet ten inches? Are smooth hands important? What about the "nice eyes" that so many women mention—could it be that they are talking about eye contact, not really eye shape or color? Are "walks on the beach" important, or do you really want a man who is going to be able to love your Saint Bernard despite its excessive slobbering? You say *no* to red-headed men even though a strawberry blond who looks like Robert Redford just walked by. You keep saying that you want a man who is funny and keep getting men who are dorky and immature. Maybe it's time to rethink your definitions.

Family Expectations

To discern the role your friends' and family's expectations and advice play, you have to ask yourself a few questions: Whom are you listening to? Do you believe that love is supposed to conquer all, or should you kick him to the curb after a certain point? Are you being realistic, or are you seeking the rags-to-riches fantasy you've grown up to believe? Is being with this man a personal quest, the challenge of doing something everyone else said not to do? Do you think that you're making a larger statement about the power of love?

Oprah Winfrey says confront him, your mom doesn't understand what the big deal is, your best friend thinks you are a doormat, the radio keeps playing sad love songs that encourage reconciliation, and you know exactly how Meredith is feeling on *Grey's Anatomy*.

His Point of View: "I Never Signed On for This"

I never agreed to go to law school, stop eating veal, or whiten my teeth! She latched on to the topic and wouldn't let it go. I heard about it morning, noon, and night. If I did it right, I got a big smile; if I did it wrong, I'd get the sad face or a tantrum."

Recognizing the Triggers

Women have their romantic soft spots, built on experiences from when they were young: things they saw their fathers do (or not do), scenes from particularly memorable romantic films, a moment from a favorite book. These items range from the deep and evocative to the superficial and frivolous. In other words, it's one thing to fantasize about a man who gives you a foot massage in bed; it's another to be moved when your boyfriend decides to volunteer at a local shelter.

What are the clichéd qualities that you believe make a good man? Do you hear yourself saying, "I know this sounds stupid, but I love that that he [fill in the blank—e.g., feeds me off his fork, calls his mother, likes my dog]." These tender moments can pack an emotional wallop, especially if you've been carrying them close to your heart for years.

Take Jenny, for instance. She reports, "The first time Antonio called me his *soul mate* when introducing me at a party, I nearly cried. I was so touched. He had some big issues, but he used a term I had always thought the man of my dreams would at least understand. He *had* to be the one."

It's understandable that after years of waiting, Jenny was emotionally triggered to hear her fantasy play out in real life—so much so that it may have been difficult for her to recognize the very real possibility that Antonio's choice of the words *soul mate* was a mere coincidence. Maybe he just saw it in a movie or heard it in a song on the way to the party. In any case, it's unlikely that it's as meaningful to him as it is to her.

Be on guard for investing too much meaning in details, even if they seem to run deeper than the spoken word. Sometimes you long for a particular ideal quality in a man, like "I wish he were more spiritual" or "I wish he would surprise me every once in a while." Of course, these are positives and should be counted, but they should not outweigh more significant concerns, like whether he has a job, is emotionally stable, or treats you well.

Susan is a good example of a case in which a relatively unimportant positive trait outweighed a lot of negatives. She said, "I had always fantasized about a guy who would say, 'Hey, I want to take a dance class. I know it's kind of a funny request, but would you consider it?' I just thought that it was the ultimate romantic thing. So when Jeff said those words, almost verbatim, even though he was all wrong, I figured it was a sign that he was the one." In retrospect, it can seem ridiculous that her internal scales were so out of whack. Dance class is nice, but is it more important than having a reliable boyfriend who makes you happy in other ways?

It can be hard to recognize when you have a trigger like this; after all, these are deep-seated emotions. You may not even realize that the tender way your boyfriend wraps your scarf around your neck when it's cold has somehow outweighed the fact that he always backs out of important events at the last minute. Ask yourself again the three questions listed earlier. Defusing these emotional land mines by becoming aware of them and examining them is one way to make sure they don't blow up in your face.

Commitment Aversion: Can It Be Changed?

What happens if a man's aversion to commitment is exactly what you want to change about him? You've been pushing for monogamy, cohabitation, or marriage, and he has resisted for any number of reasons. Understanding his lack of commitment may help you to be more patient with or sympathetic toward him—or it could just drive you crazy.

The Commitmentphobe

Commitment phobia is hardly a newly noted phenomenon among men, and it tends to have some common causes. The way everyone views romantic relationships is unavoidably and irrevocably affected by what has been witnessed and experienced in one's own family—and let's face it, most families are messed up in one way or another.

What's your guy's family like? Divorce is rather common these days; did he witness a particularly bitter one at a formative age? Did he see his parents get married and remarried? Does his father talk about how marriage ended his life? These are just a few of the ways in which negative feelings toward romantic commitment can grow from deep-seated family experiences.

Of course, not every commitmentphobe comes from a broken home. Some men simply fear the implied loss of independence and the potential loss of power that is associated with a long-term relationship of any kind. Although this could be related to family experience, such as watching Mom scream at Dad for eighteen years, most men want to be perceived as powerful, virile, and free, and monogamy can counteract these traits. Being in a committed relationship means that someone (for example, you) could call him at any time and expect him to do something: go to dinner with your parents, pick up a quart of milk, come over for dinner. Sex with other women is, of course, out.

This brings us to the consummate window shopper. Have you ever had a friend who hemmed and hawed endlessly over a particular purchase? She's been talking forever about getting a nice watch for herself, but there's always a sale around the corner or a new style coming out. There are men like this, too; they try you on, but they are always wondering if there is someone hotter, younger, richer, or whatever whom they could date instead—maybe someone who doesn't nag them so much, someone who thinks they're perfect just the way they are.

The institution of marriage can stir up especially deep resistance. For some men, it's simply the towering, irreversible lifetime commitment that drives them quietly bonkers. They will never sleep with another woman, never leave the dishes in the sink for a week, never be free to do whatever they want whenever they want. *Never.* It does sound like a real bummer when it's put that way, doesn't it? The "till death do us part" vow has a particularly ominous ring to a man who was uncomfortable with commitment to begin with and who does not want to contemplate his own mortality.

In an emotional sense, some men see marriage as the end of the self. After all, it is a union of two people, two spirits, two lives, two residences, two (or more) credit cards, and two vacation times. From here on in, all decisions will be shared with a partner. Many men also dread the added responsibility of providing for a family, knowing that this trumps personal desires.

An ICK versus a Deal Breaker

There he is, across the table. It's your first or second date, and he does that thing again—that thing that annoyed you the first time. Before you get too deeply involved, take a moment to really weigh whether this is your basic ICK response (and therefore something you can work on) or a deal breaker (and therefore you will lose his number). Whatever your rule is, take a minute and examine it. On the one hand, maybe you should be more flexible with your definition of what calls the deal off in a second; on the other hand, maybe the thing you brush off as just coincidence is a huge red flag. Look at it. It's hard to miss. Why are you missing it?

Take some time and think about how your definition of both has changed because of your experience. What friends have deal breakers that you consider ridiculous, and when have you heard that yours are silly or self-defeating, too?

Comparing Him to Your Friends' Boyfriends

Women's friendship circles are very important. For most women, their friends are an important component of emotional support. Gatherings can be a hotbed of information sharing (okay, gossip) and advice seeking. Conversations between female friends about romantic relationships can become comparative, if not downright competitive.

So your friend has convinced her pothead boyfriend to get a real career and propose to her. She cajoled and manipulated and pushed, but in the end she got what she wanted. Now you're dating an antisocial commitmentphobe, and your friend's tricks don't seem to be working their magic. In fact, nothing seems to be working. What's wrong with you? She made it seem so easy.

First, you have to accept that there's a certain amount of magical timing that goes into all of this. Your friend's tactics might not have worked if she had met that pothead a year earlier. This may sound hopelessly cliché, but project boyfriends are like snowflakes; no one formula will work for everyone. Your friend's strategy may be interesting or make for a good story, but it's not a surefire recipe for you to follow.

What If He Wants *You* to Change?

A central law of physics is that if you exert force on something, it will exert equal force back. This is also true in the project relationship. You want him to stop drinking straight out of the milk carton, but he wants you not to mind so much. Every time he does it, part of him hopes that you won't care (or won't catch him). This is the silent negotiation of relationships.

He may roll his eyes, bring up something *you* do, or say, "Sorry," as he does every time, but not mean it. You may also hear him say something about how he just wants you to be like you were when the two of you met. You didn't mention anything about table manners on the first date! You were fun and impulsive. We've talked about the early dating effect (EDE), in which everyone is on his or her best behavior. It definitely plays a role here. It's also worth considering the following, however: Are you losing spontaneity? Are you turning into his mom—or worse (gasp), yours?

Although most men miss the woman from the beginning of the relationship, you may have a guy who was hoping that he could get you to settle down, to limit your social activities and just do things with him—that is, to change *you*. This is very different from the traditional woman-wants-man-to-change scenario, but it happens. Think of the friends you know whose boyfriends want them to be more into sports, be like the other wives, or enjoy the outdoors.

Things He Does (Consciously or Unconsciously) That Make You Think "He's Got Potential"

- Underneath it all is a heart of gold. Who are these men who make you see the glass as half-full and not half-empty? They are the "stray dogs" with good manners, the passionate artists and the misunderstood poets, the calculating guys who know how to keep the scales tipping the teeniest way in their direction so that you are always doing the math and coming up with 49 percent. It's as if they're whispering in your ear, "Sure I'm too young (or old or fat or poor or mean or free-spirited), but believe in me; under it all I have a heart of gold. I'm a good person. I have potential." All of a sudden, like the subliminal message of a commercial that sends you running down the vitamin aisle to try a new supplement, you find yourself saying, "Hey, why not give it a try? What's the worst that could happen?"

  Reality: If you want a guy who underneath it all really has a heart of gold then, bingo, you've got it. If the outside is all dusty and dented, however, it might not be worth it to you. Just know that he is hinting or giving off the vibe that underneath it all he is really a diamond in the rough, so beware: the rough may never go away.

- He likes me. He really likes me. You know these guys. When they're with you, they're really into you: lots of gazing into each other's eyes, holding hands, and having earnest talks. Then suddenly the guy disappears, either literally or figuratively. He forgets things, like your birthday or to call you more than every few weeks. His excuses always sound legitimate—sort of. Whenever you try to talk to him about your concerns or about moving the relationship along, he does something like stroke your cheek and murmur,

"I really like you." And you really like him. It seems as if he's just asking you to be patient, which you can totally do! He's worth it. Besides, it's fun when you're together. If you just hang in there, he'll come around. Maybe it's later in the relationship, and whenever you try to talk to him about his flakiness or sloppiness, he says, "But *I* like *you* just as you are." This disarms you for a while, but the problem is far from solved.

Reality: This guy knows that women are rigged (neurologically) to feel as if their significant other really likes or loves the person they are deep down. It's nice to have a man say he really likes you, especially when you really like him. Nevertheless, actions speak louder than words. He may have learned this as a line and be using it exactly that way. He loves your soul, damn it—why can't you do the same? (Sobbing noises)

- "Please be patient with me; I have issues." This message is hidden in his words. It's subtle, but you hear it. He'll never say it just like that, but he'll hint, and you'll latch onto it. Doesn't everyone have issues? Your man explains that the reason he's short-tempered or antisocial or lazy is that he was bullied at school. He's messy because his domineering father always yelled at him about cleaning up his room. He's moody because he's on a new medication. You think it's nice that he can be so intimate with you; he obviously trusts and needs you. Of course, the issues he's dealing with are more significant than your petty grievances. You'll help him with his problems, and he will certainly become more calm, friendly, and active as a result of your hard work. In the meantime, you'll try to put aside your petty grievances, absorb his anger, or ignore the mess.

Reality: If he has real problems, he needs real help. Is he getting the treatment he needs, or are you subbing as a therapist? Is he reeling you in by hinting that he is problematic and not going to change, so that later you'll blame yourself? You knew he had issues; he pretty much said so. Sincere apologies also mean different things to women than they mean to men. To women they mean "I understand how you feel, and I won't do it again now that I know." To men, they mean "I really wish I hadn't done that thing that is getting me in so much trouble now."

Word to the (Now) Wise

The name of the game is reading between the lines, making sure that you don't project your expectations and get carried away with the subtle messages he is sending that seem innocuous but can be very powerful. If you dismiss certain traits or behaviors during EDE, it's your "fault," but he also has to learn to admit that he might have hinted or kept quiet when certain topics about change, opinion, or taste came up. He was so focused on keeping his eye on the prize that he just nodded and smiled.

4 Liars, Cheaters, Cheapskates, and Couch Potatoes

Enough about you. Now let's take a good look at him.

While you can list the characteristics of your Prince Charming in one breath, you also know what you're *not* looking for, and you've been around the block enough to know that love does not conquer all. In this chapter, we'll give you the real deal about different types of men so that you don't keep wasting your time. Let's face it, whatever you've been doing hasn't worked very well, has it?

First of all, your man is complex. He might fit squarely in one box (that is, be one type) or he might not (that is, he might be a mixture of types). However, if the basics of any of these descriptions ring true, it's vital that you know what you're up against—it could save you lots of time and lots of heartache.

What's the first word that comes into your mind when you're describing him? What's the one trait that overrides all others? Take an objective look at him, examining the kinds of clothes he wears (button-down shirts or T-shirts and blazers, a baseball cap or a fedora), his core group of friends, the way he communicates, and the way he talks about the other people in his life.

In all the types of men that are listed here, there are both positive and negative traits. Why else would you have become involved with such a man in the first place? He reels you in with his intensity, his charm, and his good nature, but eventually you realize that there are some wrinkles that have to be ironed out—this can mean accepting his flaws, minimizing them, or setting out to squash them once and for all. We will tell you what you need to know about the inner workings of your man, help you to understand why you got sucked in, and tell you honestly just how much the odds are stacked against you.

How Does Your Guy Rate?

A lengthy anecdotal collection of hundreds (perhaps even thousands) of accounts of men, both nationally and internationally, by friends and by patients, has led us to create a rating system that is fairly reliable. This is a good starting point. Use it along with your intuition and your personal experience to make your decision.

★ **One star or less.** This guy is probably not going to change. Yes, hell might freeze over and he might actually surprise you, but if you are holding your breath and waiting, you'll die, so it's best to exhale and move on. At the very least, set up a reasonable time frame and goals so that you don't stay on indefinitely and waste your time. Personally, we would head for the hills—fast.

★★ **Two stars.** This guy has small potential for change. Nevertheless, be careful; this is only a smidgen better than a one-star guy, so we wouldn't bet money on him. He's hard to categorize, because he will show the occasional glimmer of possibility, but then another flicker won't come for quite a while. With a lot of encouraging, pushing, and luck—in fact, mostly luck—he might budge, but be prepared to trudge along on a long, hard road that might not end where you want.

★★★ **Three stars.** This guy has fair potential for change. This is a fifty-fifty type of guy: he could go either way. You are in a dangerous situation, because he could keep you in limbo, waiting for him to tip one way or the other to help you decide whether to leave or stay. In the end, the change might have nothing to do with your efforts at all.

★★★★ **Four stars.** This man has good potential for change. That still means that there will be times when the going is rough, but it's worth sticking around for a while to see what develops. His faults are workable, he is amenable, and you won't completely lose your mind getting him from point A to point B.

★★★★★ **Five stars.** Ah, the perfect man, the one with excellent potential. He might just be the guy who even asks for your guidance. This doesn't mean that change will come fast, but it *will* come. It's up to you to find the tactic that will work or the presentation that will inspire, but hang in there, because it's just a matter of time.

Are there guys whose bad behavior doesn't even make for one star? Half? Absolutely. If he is physically violent with you, lies about having an entire family in another state, runs a dog-fighting ring in the basement, or has been arrested in numerous states, he's off the charts, as in excuse yourself to go to the bathroom and climb out the fire escape or suddenly remember you are married to the county sheriff.

The Mean Guy: Half a Star

Rationale: You have stuck with the Mean Guy so far because you can't imagine that he really understands how awful the things he does or says are. He couldn't possibly understand; otherwise, how could he be perfectly normal and sweet within minutes, even seconds, after the gaffe? All people say things they regret once in a while, but with him it's a pattern of behavior. He hurts your feelings over and over, and it's not an accident or an isolated event. He is just plain *mean*. It's hard to accept, but it's true. You check with your girlfriends, and the verdict is unanimous: *mean*.

Breakdown: The essential characteristic of this man is that he is unaware (or is good at acting as if he is) that his actions are passive-aggressive, condescending, or hurtful. Most important, he shows little or no remorse once his behavior is pointed out to him. This is a dangerous situation because the meanness can be subtle, masked by sarcasm or humor, or couched between pet names like *Honey* or *Baby*. It grows in slight increments, so your tolerance for his snide remarks or cruelty increases with time. You often don't realize exactly just how mean he is until you describe a typical incident to a friend who says, "Wow, that's really cold!"

Mean Guys are the most difficult kind of men to change. They simply find better reasons for being stressed, grouchy, annoyed, irritable, or nasty. Sometimes you think that you can just negotiate with him not to use the words that hurt you. However, he'll revert to the same facial expression, which translates into the very same phrase. He knows it, and you know it. His trademark is to flip the script to make *you* feel crazy or oversensitive so that you are left questioning yourself instead of him.

Verdict: Mean Guys never become kind. They will change how they say things, but the underlying message—that you are stupid, fat, or crazy and lucky to have landed them—remains the same. The prognosis for change is virtually zero. Most likely you will try to ignore this prognosis by donning a harder shell, trying to protect yourself from being slighted, and continuing to enjoy the good things, whatever they are. This is not only difficult but also practically impossible. Slowly, his disparaging comments will take a toll on you, whittling away at your self-esteem. Your only option is to get out.

The Jealous (and Controlling) Guy: One Star 

Rationale: We give this guy one star. He may be tolerant of your male friends when you are first dating, but he soon starts showing another side of himself, and the truth finally comes out: he doesn't believe that men and women can be friends—ever. Any man who wants to talk to you must have ulterior motives, the main one being to get into your pants. He is always on high alert when there is any male within a five-mile radius of you, whether it's your married coworker or the hot dog vendor.

Your rebuttals don't matter: "He's happily married." "We've been friends since childhood." "He's gay." "I just wanted a hot dog!" Nothing placates him. His jealousy becomes the cause of most of your arguments, and you find yourself omitting parts of your day in your conversations in order to avoid the snide comment or probing question. Other than that, he's perfect. The problem is that he wants to change you!

Breakdown: Sometimes his jealousy, once limited to your male friends, grows to include all other people.

At first it may seem protective and even sort of sweet that he wants you all to himself, but it soon begins to feel stifling and irrational. Your attempts to make him feel secure hit a brick wall. You introduce him to your friends, invite him along on everything you do, and assure him that he has no competition; then you find yourself slowly making adjustments to your life to avoid his anger. You make calls when he is in the shower and omit mentioning certain people he doesn't like when you tell a story. You keep thinking that if you could make him understand or believe in your love, he'd trust you—but that never happens. In fact, things get incrementally worse.

The bad news about this guy is that his jealousy may originate from a deep insecurity that takes lots of time and effort to heal. He may have difficulty with very basic trust issues, or his accusations against you could even be a projection of his own wandering eyes (in which case he's double trouble). Setting respectful rules that are truly compromising for both of you may be unrealistic if he is not mature or motivated.

Verdict: Is losing you motivation enough for him to change, or is his ultimate goal to steal you away and have you all to himself?

A variation of the jealous guy is the Clingy Guy. The first time he said you were his sunshine, you smiled. How sweet, you thought. You are his better half, the one who inspires him to live every day. Then you realized that he meant it—*really* meant it. If you let him out of your sight long enough, he'll come back with a tattoo of your first and last name on his neck (how could you leave him now?). He has a T-shirt made at the mall with a picture of the two of you together, and he parades you around like a handler at the Westminster dog show.

This man would take a bullet for you; in fact, he'd take a whole round to prove his love. However, if you even hint at taking a trip with "just the girls," he'll poke his lower lip out all week, skulking around like Linus without his blanket. He believes that his neediness is love and that your ambivalence is aloof and cold-hearted. Nothing makes him back off: not PMS, shoe shopping, "chick flicks," or bridal magazines. The more you ask of him and include him, the happier he is.

If you spend too much time in the bathroom, he'll be tapping on the door asking if everything is all right or if you need any toilet paper. You can't run, hide or, at this point, even breathe. Furthermore, he has no qualms about hinting that losing you would mean that life wouldn't be worth living. You find yourself hoping that you'll get a job transfer to someplace far, far away.

A subcategory of this guy is the Wounded Bird. Somehow you were the person who healed him, whether it was from a broken heart from his last girlfriend or an extra bad case of adult chicken pox.

The Cheater: One Star ★

Rationale: The reason this guy deserves any star at all is that once in a blue moon, a cheater will cheat the odds and change. Not all cheaters are serial offenders; straying once could be a mistake he regrets and from which he learns. However, if he's cheated on everyone he's ever seriously dated and only becomes upset when he's caught, then philandering is part of his personality. This is a man who wants the attention of several women, and who also likes the power play and the risk that cheating entails.

We want to make sure you know the facts, loud and clear, so that you can choose how to deal with it, whether it means policing his every move, deciding to believe that he loves you more than the other women he is seeing, or shrugging it off because you have unlimited access to his wallet. Whatever your rationale is, we won't judge. Just know that he's not trading in his Don Juan character anytime soon, if ever.

Breakdown: He has cheated on women in the past; maybe he even cheated on you, and you've decided to take him back. Does "once a cheater, always a cheater" hold true for everyone? If the mutually agreed upon rules you've made about what is permissible within your relationship have been broken, is it worth always having to look over your shoulder, questioning your intuition?

More often than not, the Cheater has found a way to make peace with his indiscretions; it is part of his definition of who he is ("I'm a free spirit," "I just love women," "I'm irresistible."). He has his excuses, which run the gamut from having an insatiable sexual appetite to claiming that as long as no one finds out, no one gets hurt. He's in a relationship and says that he's sleeping on the couch, that he and his wife or live-in girlfriend are really separated. He says that she's a bitch, that they haven't had sex in months, or that they are both seeing other people, but he is with her because of one (or all!) of the following:

- He feels bad kicking her out because she has nowhere to go.
- She owes him money, and he knows that she won't pay him back if he leaves her.
- Her mother, grandfather, stepsister, best friend, or favorite Girl Scout counselor from the fifth grade is dying, and he can't leave her now or he'd be a real jerk.

Verdict: Not all liars are cheaters, but all cheaters are liars.

The Pathological Liar: One Star ★

Rationale: For this man, lying is a habit, a knee-jerk reaction, but this doesn't make it okay—far from it. Most likely he learned how to lie as a child, and now he has it down to a science. Lying has worked for him thus far, getting him what he wants and needs, whether that is avoiding trouble or commanding attention for his wild stories. Deep down inside he might even be proud of what he gets away with; he does it often and to everyone in his life, to some degree.

Beware when you begin to discover inconsistencies in his facts or realize that you are second-guessing what he tells you. Even serious repercussions or long-term therapy might not straighten out this guy completely. Maybe you don't mind "translating" what he tells you, whether it's about money, time, or the sequence of events, but just know that having heart-to-heart talks with him about responsibility, trust, or whether his hand actually was inside the cookie jar is not going to change his actions much. You may weigh the pros and cons and decide that he still works for you, but don't confuse your ability to adapt with his ability to tell the truth.

Breakdown: How do you define a lie? Is truth an absolute for you, or is there space for all shades of gray ("not strictly the truth" or an "omission"), depending on what someone's experience of the truth is? These are all interesting philosophical questions, but when your date says, "I was working late last night," you know that that should mean he was feverishly tapping away at his computer, getting overtime pay by working a third shift, or racing around a track, if he's a NASCAR driver. The gray area starts when he was with "clients" at "dinner," and "dinner" was at a strip joint, or the "client" was also a friend and "she" finds him physically attractive.

What's to say that a pathological liar won't lie when you ask him not to do so? It was believed that little children couldn't lie, but research now shows that children as young as four know the difference between the truth and not the truth.

Lies are a touchy subject, and you have to look long and hard at your own definition of the truth. This is tricky. You want this relationship to work; he's so promising. So when the first sign appears that he has a major defect, you start to justify and rationalize because you're not ready to give up just yet; the good still outweighs the bad. The trick is to realize when the balance is tipping in the wrong direction. Truth, trust, and intuition are three hot topics in relationships. You need to be able to trust your gut. This situation is challenging. We aren't necessarily telling you to ditch him; just be realistic about what can change, and don't recalibrate your expectations.

Verdict: How do you know he's not lying when he tells you that he won't lie anymore?

The Pessimist or Complainer: One and a Half Stars 

Rationale: The Pessimist or Complainer is the man who swears that he is an undiscovered genius or is misunderstood. The Pessimist or Complainer has grown up thinking that Archie Bunker was a real person, and they might even be related. Complaining is just the way he communicates—about everything, from the weather to world events. A lesser known version is the Self-Deprecating Guy, who relies on ripping into himself as a way of connecting to others. The Pessimist or Complainer may even be a bit paranoid.

At first you are attracted to how humble he is, but then his "aw, shucks" attitude goes from self-deprecating jokes to just self-deprecating. He loves you and wants you to be at his side, but you find yourself spending most of your time trying to cheer him up, urging him to look at the bright side of things.

Breakdown: This nihilist makes Friedrich Nietzsche look like *Extreme Makeover* host Ty Pennington. "Why bother, we're all going to die anyway" is his mantra. Included in the same spectrum is the Flatliner, a guy whose emotional range has two speeds: on and off. Not even the "Christian the Lion" YouTube video makes him weepy. All disciples of Eeyore (the dismal donkey in *Winnie the Pooh*), these guys make sure they point out the downside: the glass is always half empty, the grass is greener over there, and the glory days are always back when he was in high school, college, camp, or growing up. In his view, he is giving everyone a realistic view of the world, and they should be grateful.

Verdict: He definitely has his good points, but overcoming built-in, long-term pessimism is a real challenge. This is an instance in which *you* have to be careful not to be too optimistic!

The Addict: Two Stars ★★

Rationale: Although this guy may have a five-star personality, you cannot change him—the decision to seek help is his alone. Addictions aren't just about drugs and alcohol; there are also gambling addictions, sex and pornography addictions, and even money addictions. Your pleading, bargaining, scheming, and waiting may actually enable him to continue, if you aren't careful. He has to make a commitment to recovery, with whatever treatment he chooses. At that time, you may go along with him for the ride, but you can't put him on your back and take him there yourself.

No matter how many times you explain to him that his addiction is hurting you and damaging the relationship, and you tell him about the number of avenues that are available to him for help, he has to find the motivation within himself. Run, don't walk, to a friends and family support meeting, where the people there will tell you the same thing. The light at the end of the tunnel is that he could very well be ready to make the commitment to get better now, and he wants you by his side in the process. It's up to you, however, to decide if you want to go along.

Breakdown: He drinks too much, spends too much money, parties too much. Finally there comes a day when you realize that it (whatever it is) is out of control. He might be deep in denial about his addiction and, without malicious intent, string you along with responses like the following:

- "I have control over my addiction. I have the choice to be moderate, and when I am extreme, it's because I make the conscious choice to be that way. My behavior is within the range of normal; I am still in control. You are uptight."

- "I am much better than I used to be. If you will support me, eventually I will be able to get better on my own."
- "My alcohol use, drug use, or gambling is actually helpful. It helps me to relax, be more creative, and be more introspective."
- "Before, I never had anyone to change for. Now that I have you, I have a reason to try. Be patient, you'll see."

You might have heard all of these rationales or a variation, combination, or random rotation of them. It is possible for him to change, but it is a long, hard road. If you choose to stick around for the recovery process, you need to be realistic that sobriety (no matter what the addiction) will become an issue that permeates every aspect of your relationship.

Note: Be on extra alert for excuse number 4, the one that designates you as the beacon of hope. Any addiction counselor will tell him within the first ten minutes that this is manipulative at best: it is the wrong reason and, frankly, it just doesn't work.

Verdict: There's only one person who can decide to get him into recovery, and it isn't you.

The Couch Potato: Two Stars 

Rationale: Your guy might be too tired to jump out of bed for a morning run, too lazy to go out to grab the groceries from the car, and too much of a bum to clean up after himself, but he's not a completely lost cause. You may be able to inspire your man to be a more active participant in his life, but it's not going to be easy. Ambition lights a fire under some people, but it scares others so much that they're satisfied with a stress-free life in which the hardest question of the day is "Who has the remote?"

Then again, one could argue that ambition is part of one's genetic makeup: either you have it or you don't. Others point to life circumstances: if you *have* to work for it, you will. Maybe your guy is adorable and trustworthy, but his favorite pastime is channel surfing and ordering takeout. He may sleep till noon no matter what time he goes to bed, and when you ask him what his plans for the day are, he points to the dishes in the sink that have been there over a week and mutters, "Those."

Let's cut to the chase:

1. Is he teaching you to slow down and smell the roses and not to sweat the small stuff, or is he dragging you down with him?
2. Is he lazy, or is he clinically depressed?
3. How important to you is it that you have a partner who is like you in terms of energy level?
4. Does his low-simmer attitude extend to his life goals?
5. He might choose not to train for a marathon with you, but will he show up to cheer you on?

Breakdown: The Couch Potato does have his appeal. After all, who doesn't love snuggling? That's a great activity when it's cold, dark, or raining. Fast-forward to the first day of spring, however, and you're hyper, ready to go out and enjoy the nice sunny days. There's air in your bike tires, and you're ready to ride. You have things to do, people to see, life to celebrate. He, however, is dozing. He pulls you back onto the bed. "Five more minutes," he mumbles, but you know that this means half an hour or even an hour or two. You lie there with your eyes wide open, pinned down by an arm, going through your mental checklist of what you have to get done that day. The clock is ticking, the sun is shining, and he is fast asleep.

One day you read about the symptoms of depression in men, and you realize that these are totally descriptive of your guy: low energy, no motivation, inability to focus. "Hey, that's my Couch Potato!" If it's a depressive or an anxiety disorder that has him trapped under the covers, he has to get professional help. If he's slow moving, he has to pick up the pace every once in a while. If he's downright lazy, leave him in the dust.

Verdict: Is he a homebody, or does he need a psychological intervention? Either way, he has to get off the couch or you'll start resenting him big-time.

A modern variation of the Couch Potato is the Computer Potato: he spends all day refreshing his Facebook page, instant messaging with his friends, and watching YouTube videos. Does he need groceries? He orders from Fresh Direct. Does he want to watch a movie? He uses Netflix, of course. He doesn't watch sports, but he does dedicate hours a day to playing fantasy football.

Of course, video games are part of the problem, as well. Before dinner, he's playing World of Warcraft. After dinner, it's right back to the computer (while you clean up) catching up on Twitter. At this rate, he'll be twenty pounds overweight by the end of the year unless you replace the desk chair with a stationary bike, or better yet, surprise him with a Nintendo Wii Fit. Why go out, he believes, when you have menus online, friends online, discussions online, and videos online? Lately, you've found that the best way to get his attention is by sending sexy pictures to his e-mail, with messages like "Hey, you, I'm naked, why don't you turn around?"

Another variation of the Computer Potato is the Electronic Guy. He shows little enthusiasm for anything that doesn't have to be plugged in or run on batteries. Nothing makes him emote more than the news that an updated version of a great gadget is on the horizon. All of his calls and e-mails focus on the positives and negatives of the newest handheld something-or-other. He'll talk to customer service, blog on forums, and subscribe to the *Hacker Quarterly*. His screen name is something like RickRoll. The last time he wrote you a poem, you had to translate it from binary code.

Verdict: Is he a Bill Gates in the making, or is his world limited to a screen or an instruction manual? If he can't learn to develop at least a few flesh-and-blood interactions with you and other human beings face-to-face, you may find your attention starting to wane.

The Poet, Artist, or Musician Wannabe: Three Stars ★★★

Rationale: We give this man three stars. He plays with your head and runs circles around your heart, but he is a great seducer. Temperamental and spontaneous, he is all or nothing. When he's "on" and he has the spotlight shining on you, you feel special and loved, but when he's distracted by work or uninspired, you wonder what you've done wrong. The intermittent reinforcement of his attention—think slot machines—gets you hooked.

One of the main characteristics of this type is narcissism or self-centeredness: he is convinced that he deserves fame, whether it's as an actor, a painter, or a bassist. You find yourself asking, "What happens if he doesn't make it? And if he does make it, will he keep me at his side?" He'll never stop defining himself as an artist, but his chronological age, erratic income, and a couple of hard knocks of reality will temper his obsession with making it big. Not everyone can be Botticelli, Bono, or Brad Pitt. Can he change from a one-man show to a solid romantic partner?

Breakdown: He's tortured, talented, obsessed with his art, on the brink of being homeless, and with no plan B. Maybe he's selling some paintings or poems or knows that a record company is going to give him a deal—next week. He may have the same ten friends at his gigs every week or think that his poetry will sell posthumously. His passion still intrigues you, nonetheless. His love of art gives him a sensitive side. He's fragile, misunderstood, and, at times, arrogant. He's also addicted to the notion of fame—or just recognition in his circle of artists. He would never "sell out" and get a job; he's "keeping it real." Is he a real artist, or is he just stalling so that he doesn't have to grow up?

Ask yourself the following:

- Does he work every day on his craft? Or is he always "working it out in his head"?
- Has he ever had a steady job to support himself? Or does he rely on the charity of others (and you)?
- Will he take any little art-related job, or are most "beneath" him?

Being in a relationship with an artist can be exciting in terms of surprises and spontaneity—both good and bad. Today, you're his muse; tomorrow, however, you might be inhibiting his creativity. (And who knows? Maybe he *will* be discovered. Then his fantasies of fame and adoration may come true, and you'll have another slew of problems to deal with!) Regardless, fasten your seatbelt; it's going to be a bumpy ride! You don't want to be a killjoy or be left with a "would-have, could-have," self-pitying kind of guy, but if he can learn to be more grounded and consistent, it will help your sanity a lot.

Verdict: The randomness and unpredictability of his attention gets you hooked. He's passionate and temperamental, but he's driving you nuts. It's a toss-up!

The Know-It-All: Three Stars ★★★

Rationale: No matter what the person sitting across from him at dinner has done (even if it is your brother or a friend's husband), he suddenly morphs into the expert on the subject and can one-up him or her. You listen to him while gritting your teeth, wishing he'd ask a question or give the other person a few tips and then just shut up and stop competing.

Breakdown: Your easygoing man professes that he knows how make the best omelet ever, knows how to take the shortest route anywhere, and has recovered himself from every injury, accident, or bite known to humanity. You find yourself making excuses for his overexuberance.

Verdict: Does his criticism diminish as he gets more comfortable? Lessen as he changes jobs and is happier in life? Or does the out-of-this-world sex make his rantings just background noise you can get used to? Or the opposite, your once-full dinner parties start dwindling and it becomes you as audience of one to his thumbs up or thumbs down evaluations of everything. Another three-star toss-up!

This guy comes in the following different flavors:

- *The Snob.* Maybe he did have the best sushi at Nobu on Crystal Cruises on the way to Dubai, or maybe most of his knowledge of everything comes from having taken notes while watching *Lifestyles of the Rich and Famous.* Part Dr. Frasier Crane and part Professor on *Gilligan's Island*, he is yearning for cravats to make a comeback.
- *The Intellectual.* If he's not critiquing a PBS documentary, he's paraphrasing the brilliant author of a study published in an academic journal. Part Dr. Spock and part Alistair Cook, he causes your friends to clam up around him, for fear of sounding stupid.
- *The Critic.* Whether it's the latest *American Idol* contestant or the appetizers you've just served, this man's style is to rank everything on a scale of one to ten. He's Simon Cowell on steroids—nothing can just *be*, it has to have upsides and downsides, strengths and weaknesses, and it has to be compared to previous encounters, whether it's wine or the latest movie.
- *The Indignant/Ethics Guy.* He is either irritated or indignant. When he's behind the wheel of a car, everyone driving in front of him is an idiot, and his sarcastic comments about

"Mr. Einstein" or "that genius over there" are in every other sentence. He's the one who's outraged by bad parking, customer service, or the lack of fairness of every situation. Since he seems to have missed his calling as a Court TV judge, he has redirected his wrath on everyone from waitresses to newscasters.

The Cheapskate: Three Stars ★★★

Rationale: This guy fits the bill (pardon the pun) for what you want, except for the fact that he has the slowest wallet-draw in the United States of America. Everyone skimps to save money at some time or another, but the amount of money he spends has no direct correlation to how much he makes. It is rooted in the belief that he should not be parted from his hard-earned dollar.

There are all kinds of cheapskates, from the ones who complain about the price of everything in general to those who are very situation-specific. Does he roll his eyes at your spending, directly or indirectly telling you that you are extravagant and/or stupid for paying for things that you enjoy? (This man is very different from the one who is cheap with himself but not with you.) Is he embarrassing with his public calculating and bartering (and is it something he sort of enjoys, or is it rooted in the suspicion that everyone is trying to rip him off)? Unfortunately for you, the penny pinching could pervade other aspects of his life and ultimately affect your relationship. If you can resolve his issues with money, can work around them, are able to ignore them, or can reach a compromise, he'll be just about perfect. He has some potential for change, but it's not going to be a picnic getting him there.

Breakdown: How he justifies his frugality is important. It is helpful for you to understand why he behaves this way:

- He's saving money for a good reason, like a down payment on a house or a big vacation.

- He doesn't make as much as you do, and he skimps because he just doesn't have it.
- He's afraid of going broke.

Just as important, how does it make *you* feel?

- "It makes me feel as if I'm not good enough to spend money on."
- "It makes me feel as if what I want doesn't matter to him."
- "It makes me feel as if the time he is with me isn't worth it, as if he is saving for something better."

Understanding how he grew up can help you to be more patient with this kind of guy. Was his dad a gambler who didn't leave enough money for the rest of the family? Was his mom a shopaholic who never saved enough to send him to camp? Did his parents instill in him a fear of poverty or make him feel guilty for excessive spending?

Ultimately, you need to figure out how his thriftiness can negatively affect your relationship. Will he be cheap with his love and attention? Will he be stingy around your family? Is he going to be able to spend the extra buck to meet you in the middle?

Verdict: He has a fair amount of potential, but you have to figure out if there is wiggle room for this hot topic in your relationship so that you can make some informed decisions about whether it's worth it for you to hang in there.

The Pervert: Three Stars ★★★

Rationale: We give this guy three stars because he can be encouraged to screen his lewd thoughts. Again, it's fifty-fifty. Figuring out the specific scenarios and words that trigger him could help him to tone things down a little; so could the prospect of losing you. Maybe he's been taught that this is how virile men act, or that it's what women *really* want. Maybe he's just ruled by his desire for sex. The problem is that he equates how much sex you give him with how much you like him or are attracted to him, and he expects that the two of you will have as much sex a year into the relationship as you had in the beginning.

This man comes in two varieties: Type A talks a lot about sex, and when he's not talking directly about it, he's hinting at it, alluding to it, and joking about it. He rhymes words with *sex* or genitalia or anything related to them. Type B may or may not have the qualities of Type A, but he has a continual erection, which becomes more and more annoying as the relationship progresses. He professes that he is stellar in bed and could easily be a money-making gigolo if his career as a lawyer turns out to be a bust.

Breakdown: Type A is the guy who inspired the *Austin Powers* film series. Usually, you get mixed up with this kind of guy because you met him in a bar, where his oversexed behavior was somewhat sanctioned, and you probably didn't hear half the innuendos he muttered. He definitely has other redeemable qualities, which make this adolescent behavior tolerable. Maybe you try to ignore it and hope the big penis jokes will fade, but that might never happen, since he is both the actor and the audience of his own lewd jokes (especially if he changes voices).

Every time you've had enough, he does something sweet, looks inordinately handsome, or splurges on a dinner, and you think, "Hmm, maybe I can curb this man, just a little." Most adults still giggle at silly lewd jokes, which is why they like *The Simpsons* and *Family Guy*. Sometimes it's exactly this type of spontaneity that initially attracted you to this man. He seems childlike and unfazed by rules, which are qualities you wish you had sometimes (when it's appropriate).

Then, however, you realize that he doesn't turn it off. You're in the middle of an intense discussion in which you are explaining the inner pain of abandonment, and he snorts and points, "Look at her huge ass!" At a reputable awards dinner, he disregards all the recipient's outstanding achievements, whispering about her "rack." Puns are his favorite game. He stutters his laugh like Beavis and crows, "She said *titillate*, get it? *Tit*-il-late." The list is endless—at least it seems that way.

Type B can't get enough, and it's the only thing on his mind. You can't walk up the stairs in front of him without his trying to put his hand underneath your skirt. At parties, he's grinding up against you and making comments about your breasts in front of other people. In the beginning, you think you've met your sexual match. You have sex in the bed, on the sofa, on the kitchen table. Food is no longer nutrition but a sex accessory. Before long, you're sneaking into public bathrooms and disappearing into closets at friends' houses for a quickie. You've never felt so attractive in your life. Before long, however, sex is the most important thing in the relationship; in fact, it *is* the relationship.

Verdict: If you could just get the bigger brain on top to function at a higher level than the smaller brain down below, this could work. Whether it's a tolerable amount or degrading is your call. Draw the line in concrete, not sand, and stick by what is within your comfort zone.

The Man-Child: Three and a Half Stars ★★★½

Rationale: He should have grown out of this stage by now, but for some reason, he's a walking case of arrested development. The next stage in life is to be a responsible, gracious grownup, and sometimes it seems that he is almost getting there, but then his friends or adolescent fantasies pull him back down to acting like your little brother rather than doting-spouse material.

Does he still keep in touch with his fraternity brothers? Is his idea of a good time crushing beer cans on his forehead? Being a frat boy doesn't have to be a bad thing. Maybe you like the way a guy looks in a baseball cap and khakis. The fact that his frat brothers are important to him could indicate that he has a strong sense of loyalty. Nevertheless, this extreme form of male bonding can backfire if he holds steadfast to the crude "bros before hos" fraternity pledge.

The Man-Child is also the Eternal Bachelor or the Mimbo, two subtypes that cannot coexist with being a responsible adult or age-appropriate partner. He uses phrases like "he pulled the trigger" instead of "he got married." He's commitment-phobic, for the most part, measuring his self-worth by his sexual conquests. Always having been fairly good looking, he might have paid less attention to his intellectual development. This narcissist isn't necessarily immature, but he truly is in a state of arrested development.

He's so handsome, however, that you find yourself watching him sleep. As he talks (about what, who knows), you wonder how anyone's face could be so symmetrical. His lips, his teeth, his nose—you are so taken by his looks that you are able to put aside the fact that he has been yammering about the weather nonstop since you met him. Every time you think about breaking up, one of your girlfriends tells you how dreamy he is, so you figure you'll give him another week.

You also may find that there are some topics of conversation that are way over his head (global warming, the nuclear situation in North Korea), so be prepared for blank stares and a "who really cares" attitude. The Eternal Bachelor is often the party animal in his group of friends. Married men seek him out to remind them of their single days, and he's always in the wedding party of one of his buddies.

Breakdown: You are probably attracted to this guy because of his joie de vivre. He is exuberant and unapologetically loud—qualities you'd probably like to have, though in moderation. Then it hits you like a ton of bricks: when he should be solemn and calm, respectful and attentive, or sensitive and comforting, he will find a reason to put his fist in the air and make barking noises or yell things like "Yeah, baby!" You are baffled about why he can't manage to be both a college throwback and a good boyfriend. Why can't he be "one of the boys" and your boyfriend simultaneously?

Here are a few key characteristics of the Man-Child:

- Plans with guy friends cannot be broken—ever.
- You feel as if you know all his friends intimately, even though you haven't spent much time with them, because stories about his glory days infiltrate every conversation, regularly.
- His loyalty to bands, sports teams, politics, and porn stars is shared with equal fervor by his friends.
- Dancing is something he does only as a five-minute prelude to making out with a woman in a bar or at a wedding (and with his tie on his head).

A subcategory of this complex animal is the Sports Nut. There's a room in his house that's dedicated to his favorite basketball team, and when the Dallas Cowboys lose, his house takes on the aura of a funeral home. As soon as football season is over, he's glued to basketball. It doesn't matter if it's college or professional. Once March Madness is over, he's on to baseball.

It'll take a wedding or a funeral to get him out of his favorite jersey. If he's not watching sports or reading the sports section of the newspaper, then he very well may be playing one sport or another. There are many advantages to a man who has a passion, as long as it takes a middle path (and one of them doesn't include fantasy football).

Do you answer yes to any of the following questions?

1. Do you have to be home from your date by eleven o'clock to catch Sportscenter, even though he's seen all of the games that it's recapping?

2. When his team loses, is it as if he's lost his childhood pet all over again?
3. Is he spending hours in sports bars, chugging beers and fighting opposing fans?
4. On the day of a game between the New York Yankees and the Boston Red Sox, will he refuse to wear red and white?
5. Does he talk about the players, coaches, and managers as if he knows them?

If you answer *yes* to at least two, you've got a Sports Nut on your hands.

Verdict: His behavior is not malicious, just embarrassing, and you keep waiting for him to grow up. Part of the problem is that you have to come to terms with your ambivalence about squashing his childlike exuberance when everybody else considers him the life of the party. Nevertheless, you *do* have to come to terms with it, have him commit to changing his behavior, or move on.

The Self-Proclaimed ADD Guy: Four Stars ★★★★

Rationale: On dates one through ten you are mesmerized. He greets the staff of the sake bar in Japanese; he can surf, snowboard, and ice-skate; he can build a fire using dental floss and gum wrappers; and he turns your napkin into an origami swan and loves magic tricks. Unfortunately, that is all he knows. This makes for a great first couple of dates, but then he runs out of party tricks and you realize that he knows nothing in depth and actually prides himself on having what he calls vocational attention deficit disorder (ADD).

Breakdown: His enabling parents often agree with each other that his being so talented at so many things is a curse, of sorts: if only he'd been more focused, he probably could have finished college and stuck with that first, second, or third job—it's a good thing that Dad's company seems to always need extra help in supervision when he gets back from his latest surfing trip. He shrugs off jobs, saying that they weren't challenging enough, that he was bored or overqualified, or that the boss felt threatened by his natural talent. He has never actually read an entire book, but he has read the book review or seen the movie—that counts, right?

Verdict: You find his childlike excitement both adorable and infuriating at the same time. The evening flies by or drags you by the heels. You have to bite the bullet with this guy, despite his potential. It won't take *that* much on his part, but he has to put in the work.

The Undomesticated Guy: Four and a Half Stars

Rationale: He might have the basics, or he might be a totally feral man who gives the impression of having grown up in the wild, raised by a pack of wolves. Maybe he has just lived a sheltered life or grew up in the backwoods somewhere. The main concern here is to encourage him to be more open-minded. It's a fight to convince him to put on a clean shirt and jeans (the ones *without* the holes), and when you ask him what he wants for dinner, he'll grunt and say some sort of red meat—no vegetable, complex carb, or dessert.

Worst of all, hygiene is not his strong point. You once mentioned that he might want to trim his hair, but he just looked at you as if you had three heads. Teeth-whitening is inconceivable. Most probably this man categorizes topics by sex: the ones that are understandable to him ("guy stuff") and the things he doesn't have to know too much about ("chick stuff"). Anything related to women causes his eyes to glaze over, but he'll often pretend to understand in order not to have to give what he considers a long-winded reason. He is probably parroting his father's domestic survival technique.

Breakdown: This guy describes himself as a "man's man" or an "alpha male." He prefers a nice cold beer to your pinot noir, and he says that mixed greens are for rabbits. You've recognized his heart of gold and appreciate his strong family values, but his odd fork and knife grip and high level of testosterone make you apprehensive about introducing him to your friends.

There is definitely an upside, however. He didn't bat an eye the time you went on vacation to Tulum and left your razor at home. He's as reliable as the day is long and would never look at another woman. He has his friends, but you still rate number one in his book.

Verdict: He has strong potential, but he has some serious work to do. You two do not live in a cave in the wilderness, and the sooner he steps over into civilization, the better for the relationship. He may respond to a well-worded ultimatum, but you have to stick to your guns.

The Blue-Collar Guy: Four and a Half Stars ★★★★½

Rationale: We give this guy four and a half stars. He might simply need some adjustments, and he very well might surprise you—a lot depends on his personal open-mindedness and his motivation to win you. Just because he has a blue-collar job and hasn't been exposed to a wide range of experiences or a cosmopolitan lifestyle doesn't mean that he can't learn to appreciate the finer things in life. Although you may love the guy in a uniform at your friend's bachelorette party, you also might find that this real-life hard-working fella needs exposure to the finer things in life to be able to hang with you.

Breakdown: He thinks your taste is expensive and sophisticated because you like sushi and know a couple of words in French and Italian. At first, you think it's cute that he says *fox* when he really means *faux* and spells *psyched* s-i-k-e-d. He brags that he hasn't read a book since the fourth grade—he's never heard of Marcel Proust or John Grisham or even Dr. Seuss, for that matter. Who cares? He'd take a bullet for you, and that has you swooning.

The words you'd use to describe him include *sweet*, but hardly *suave*. When your friends ask you about him, you say, almost defensively, "He has street smarts and common sense and would never let anything happen to me." You have fun with him, he makes you laugh, and you know that if anything goes wrong in the house, he'll fix it without bragging about it for a week.

At certain moments, however, such as when someone mentions a good book or an article, you want to die when he nonchalantly quips, "I'm not much of a reader" or "I don't like that fancy stuff." You try to explain to him that it has nothing to do with his level of education, SAT scores, or grade point average, but that documentaries, plays, musicals, museums, and reading are fun!

Maybe instead of another issue of *Road and Track*, he could pick up the new issue of *Newsweek*. Maybe he'll read your favorite David Sedaris short story or *Ultramarathon Man* by Dean Karnazes because of the sports element. You prod him to consider the *New York Times*; he flips through the stack, chooses the automobile and real estate sections, and takes those with him to the bathroom.

Verdict: Give in a little; above all, resist the urge to roll your eyes. A motivated Blue-Collar Guy has some decent potential.

Three Variations

Three less well known types of guys are:

- *The Shy Guy*. Behind closed doors he sings, dances, and does impersonations from Arnold Schwarzenegger to Homer Simpson. The moment you step outside, your chatty guy becomes mute and gives only one-word answers in group situations. Any attempt to persuade him to join the festivities, participate in the conversation, or pretend that he is having fun fall short. You find yourself apologizing to people for his shyness and promising that they'll see the charming side of him soon enough. Unless they have a hidden camera at home, however, it's not going to happen.

- *The Family Guy.* No matter what you are doing, he has no qualms about inviting others along. "The more, the merrier" is his motto—even on days you've designated as date time. Every event turns into a group outing. Although his "just pile in" attitude is adorable when you first start dating—everyone loves Mr. "Scootch over, we have plenty of space"—he makes everyone feel special except you. You find that you are feeling like a killjoy, wishing that every date didn't have to include his family, your family, friends, friends of friends, or work buddies.
- *Mr. Money.* This guy is always assessing the value of something. Is it worth what it cost? At times you're wondering if you're sleeping with Jim Kramer instead of the man you love. Did you get a bargain, or did you get ripped off? He negotiates, barters, and can talk only about topics related to cash or credit. His motto is "Everything in life has a price on it."

Hybrids

Ben and Jerry's brilliant joining of ice cream flavors, like Bananas on the Rum (banana ice cream with a buttery rum brown-sugar swirl), is brilliant. Fruit hybrids such as the pluot (a plum and an apricot), the spork (a spoon with fork tines), and the Toyota Prius are great inventions, but the buck stops there. Use the same logic with your boyfriend and you get a Frankenstein blend of a sports nut who is also a cheapskate, a computer nerd who is also a pill popper, or an ever-popular philandering artist who is also a pervert.

The most common hybrids (and the easiest to spot) are as follows:

- *The Complainer-Cheapskate.* It is not a stretch to assume that the man with the glass-half-empty outlook on life has the same views about his money disappearing right before his very eyes. Life has handed him a plate of lemons and he has made—lemons. Although it's logical that the man who thinks he is going to die anyway would have a loose grip on his purse strings (who needs money when you're dead?), the unfortunate reality is that the same anxiety that pulsates through the Complainer can also turn him into a miser. You can pinpoint this common hybrid the first time you spend more than an hour with the man.
- *The Pessimist-Artist.* Again, it takes no stretch of the imagination to see a musician who never really got into his groove or a painter who is suffering from creative block. They would both be of the mind that society is not ready for their genius. This "screw the world" mentality coupled with a conflicting crisis of identity is quite common.
- *The Artist-Addict.* This guy could be the drummer in the local bar's cover band who has a penchant for Johnnie Walker Black, or he could be a recently published poet whose sex addiction is now being fulfilled by literary groupies. The unfortunate reality is that those who are prone to narcissistic tendencies, like artists (but keep in mind that not *all* artists fall into this category), are more likely to have addictive personalities. The result can be disastrous.
- *The Artist–Couch Potato.* This might sound counterintuitive, but the artist who has a streak of shy guy and can create from the comfort of his sofa is common. Throw in a bit of

pessimism, and he'll be the guy who's messing up your sleep schedule and making you read up on conspiracy theories.

Notes on the Hybrid Guy

1. Don't be fooled by his outward appearance. You may mistakenly think that you have a simple one-issue kind of guy, espccially on the first few dates. His ex might have broken up with him because of his being cheap, pessimistic, or immature, so he could be trying to keep that in check.
2. Go on gut instinct. If the little birdie in your head is chirping away and your stomach is sending you signals, then the chances are that you have a doozy on your hands. Women do "thin slice" really well (make up their minds about another person within the first few minutes of meeting), but when it comes to matters of the heart, women tend to dismiss their intuition. Don't.
3. Do the math. A good indication of a difficult hybrid is one who combines two low-scoring types, such as Mean Guy plus Cheater. It will take hell freezing over for a change to occur.

Test Your Type Recognition

See if you can identify the types in these scenarios. Hint: Some scenarios may have more than one answer.

Scenario 1: The dinner check comes, and he studies it. You watch him calculating in his head. Although at first he might seem to be a cheapskate, wanting to be exact to the penny, the fact that he adds, "The waitress's service was really subpar; I'd tip her the usual 15 percent, but it's just the *principle* of it that irks me" leads you to realize that he really has the tendencies of a ______________.

(continued)

Scenario 2: You know that his bragging about his knowledge of Bordeaux is not due to the wine tour he took last year but rather comes from his copy of *Wine for Dummies* next to the toilet. When you mention it, he scoffs that it wasn't really a lie; it was just a stretch of the truth, since he plans to go next year. This ability to morph time and space is not mental flexibility. What you have here is a ______________.

Scenario 3: If only he stopped his yapping and got off his rear end, he'd be perfect. Most of his monologues are on what he plans to do and never on what he is doing presently. Not only that, the plans change every day. What doesn't change is that he's always on his rump on the sofa deliberating about it. You're so desperate for him to get his act together that you're willing to sacrifice your own needs by unsubscribing to cable for a month just to see if it will help to push him out the door. Looks like you have a ______________ on your hands.

Answers: 1. Cheapskate; 2. Know-It-All Ethics Guy, Pathological Liar; 3. Couch Potato, Self-Proclaimed ADD Guy.

What You Now Know

Maybe your guy deserves an extra half star more than we gave him—or maybe half a star less. He might even be the exception to the rule who blows everyone's mind when he does a complete 180-degree turn all on his own. We hope he is that kind of guy. If he's not, however, it means accepting his flaws, minimizing them, or setting out to squash them once and for all. You'll have to see just how much the odds are stacked against you and make your own decision from there. If he fits in two boxes, that doesn't mean they average out—the good stuff is still wonderful, but the bad is exponentially harder to work with.

Now you've got his type more or less figured out. Read on as we figure out what to do with him, or rather, what not to do.

5

The Bad Boy

The Bad Boy deserves his very own chapter. Why is taming the Bad Boy such a thrill for so many women? These guys are practically covered with red flags, but when one of them swaggers into the room, certain women go weak in the knees. Men don't have to be sporting a leather jacket with a just-off-the-bike look—and they don't even have to be good-looking—to fall into the Bad Boy category, but they tend to share a few characteristics: they are unpredictable, adventurous, and looking for trouble, and they often have a reputation for being unconventional, irreverent, or confrontational. They can be self-obsessed and impulsive and have a short fuse. In other words, everything about them screams "Danger, danger!"

How *bad* a Bad Boy is depends on who you are and what you consider risqué behavior. The Bad Boy label simply means that he goes against the grain of what your family and your friends envision for you in a man. If you've always been into etiquette and he regularly scoffs at social conventions, you've got a Bad Boy on your hands. If you obsess for months about the tiny tattoo on your shoulder and he's got new ink on his skin every month, he's a Bad Boy.

What, you may ask, is so attractive about a man who is not at all what you are supposed to be looking for? Women with a taste for Bad Boys are generally the ones who most want to change a guy. He inspires more fantasies than any other man. In the stories you tell yourself, you are the special one who can make him reassess his priorities. Because of you, he will trade in his motorcycle for a Prius. He will learn to be punctual and make an effort to be polite, at least at your sister's wedding. He will limit his acquisition of new tattoos to an annual event. He will, he will, he will. Does this sound familiar?

Looking forward to a future with a reformed Bad Boy can be like getting ensnared in a big, gooey booby trap. It doesn't matter whether there's only the smallest improvement (or none at all), some women keep coming back again and again, only to suffer more disappointments. Is it torture that you keep volunteering for, or is there something else there that keeps you with him? When is the reformed Bad Boy a mirage, and when is he a real possibility?

Who Is Your Bad Boy?

Think of your favorite celebrity Bad Boy. Is he musician Tommy Lee or rapper Fifty Cent, or is he more like singer and songwriter Pete Doherty? Did the now reformed actor Colin Farrell get you going, or do you prefer more of an undercover specimen like Jude Law? How about football player Terrell Owens or actor Russell Crowe? Now think of what qualities this famous Bad Boy has that you find attractive. Figuring out what it is about him that attracts you should help to inform you of what you're after.

Russell Crowe. This Hollywood Bad Boy was known for his short temper, boozing, and brawling. In 2005, Crowe was arrested in New York City for throwing a telephone at a hotel employee. He chalked up the incident to a short temper and the tendency to respond in the moment. Now in his forties, the Aussie actor has traded in drunken late nights for parenthood. Aw, how sweet.

Bad Boy characteristic: Troublemaker, party animal.

Sean Penn. Ex-husband of Madonna, he married Robin Wright and has two Oscars to his name. Nevertheless, this notorious Bad Boy (he even starred in a movie of the same name!) has not given up his hard partying ways and his love of guns. Even as he closes in on fifty, Penn has shown no intention of changing his ways anytime soon.

Bad Boy characteristic: Rebel.

Crash-and-Burn Potential

With the Bad Boy's suitcase so full of negative traits, one would think that the average smart woman (that is, you) would steer clear of such men. However, science has now proven what most people knew yet never wanted to admit: that there is something in the Bad Boy DNA that is attractive to women. A recent study in *New Scientist* ("Bad Boys Really Do Get the Most Girls") described a "dark triad" of masculine traits—narcissism, recklessness, and deceit—that statistically translated into more sexual "conquests." Women are not just putting up with Bad Boys, they're falling for them left and right. It seems that men who are callous and obsessed with themselves tend to have more sexual partners for shorter periods than their nice guy counterparts.

Whether it's because of the thrill of vicarious living or a primal urge to feel protected, most women will find themselves in the sway of a Bad Boy at some point in their lives. The reasons may vary, but the bottom line is the same: you like them even though you know you shouldn't, even though you know the situation has very high crash-and-burn potential.

Figuring out why you like a Bad Boy is critical; determining why you are attracted (or even addicted) to him will help to kick-start your detox, facilitate your decision to stay or go, or just make you feel more in control of your life and your choices.

The Bad Boy Attraction

There are five reasons that you might like a Bad Boy. Which rings a bell with you?

Reason 1: You Are Addicted to the Suspense

Bad Boys are built to attract and sustain your romantic interest. Whether they are brooding or quick-witted, charming or reckless, most Bad Boys reel in women by alternating between attention and lack of interest. This is especially true if the guy has been paying lots of attention to you but then ignores you, and it seems as if you have faded into the background.

This erratic behavior not only lends to and maintains his air of mystery, it also hooks you in as if you were a gambler at a slot machine. It's what psychologists call *intermittent reinforcement*: you get a reward just often enough to make you keep coming back. You find yourself sitting at your desk at work, spending the entire day wondering: Will he show up on time, or will he completely forget that you had plans? Will he be nice to your friends at the bar or sulk in a corner? It is this push and pull that keeps a smart woman like you on the edge of her seat.

This unpredictability can play out in even more extreme ways. Since most people want what they can't have, some Bad Boys cultivate the sense that they could, at any moment, turn on their heels and flee. This implicit threat of rejection can infuse your whole relationship. You don't know if you're coming or going. For example, last weekend you spent forty-eight hours in bed together, sleeping, having sex, and sharing intimate secrets. Then on Sunday night he told you that he's not built for relationships and needs his space. It's disorienting and inspires a knee-jerk reaction to hold on to him for dear life.

An even more extreme Bad Boy trait is a bad temper. Since he's sensitive and unpredictable, the slightest thing can set him off and send you off on a quest to soothe him. Whether he has a high-energy gig or a mundane nine-to-five job, a bad day will likely turn into an excuse to get drunk and fight. Maybe he's a wall puncher or a moody brooder. It's easy to mistake this sort of behavior for passion, strength, and virility.

By definition, Bad Boys are womanizers. The man may be faithful to you now, but he has notches on both sides of his belt that remind you he'll never be lonely, with or without you. Whether it seems that women are buzzing around him waiting for you to walk away or you just find yourself feeling suspicious, your jealousy and feelings of insecurity are a result of his erratic behavior.

You find yourself having extreme feelings—whether bad or good. What a passionate relationship! It must be love, right? Wrong. Frustration with his bad behavior can lead to fights, and then the makeup sex is great. You reassure yourself that things will change as soon as he gets all this out of his system.

The erratic, unpredictable guy may be the most habit-forming of all the Bad Boys. He can excite you or infuriate you and make himself your obsession. Perhaps he offers up excuses for his behavior, and you really want to believe his explanations. Because he's playing you like his guitar, it can be hard to leave him.

Do I Have a Bad Boy?

He doesn't have to wear a leather jacket and smoke to be a Bad Boy; he can have a high-powered job or no job at all. It's about being a rebel. Want to be sure? Then ask yourself:

- Are you constantly worried that he's going to break up with you?
- Does part of you like the excitement? Do you find yourself saying that other guys are boring?
- Have you had to apologize for him to your friends?
- Do you feel as if you are on the edge of your seat in the relationship, always wanting more but never getting enough?
- Do you describe him as having a devil-may-care attitude, a tough guy who has overcome odds?

If you find yourself answering yes to more than half of these questions, you definitely have a Bad Boy on your hands.

Reason 2: You Feel a Special Connection with Him

"Jim drank a lot and did his fair share of drugs. He was always up for a road trip. He could never plan anything and was really spontaneous. When I was late for work or called in sick, it was usually something to do with him—either we had run out of gas or he had gotten caught up in something."

Another common factor in the romantic success of Bad Boys everywhere is that they make it seem as if they are showing you, and only you, some special part of themselves that others aren't allowed to see. Maybe it's a certain sweetness, a soft side, or a kind streak that you see in this man. So you stick up for him, both to your friends and to your own internal doubting voice. He's rough around the edges and a little short-tempered sometimes, but then there's the way he played with a dog or the fact that he teared up when he told you how traumatized he was when his favorite aunt died.

A man this deep certainly can't be expected to behave like everyone else, you tell yourself. The whole wide world misunderstands him—the whole world except for you. You are the only one who sees the soft, kind heart beneath the shell of bravado. How could you not feel sympathy for this troubled soul? Only you know how vulnerable he is—this little boy who is always mistaken for something harder. Since you are privy to an otherwise totally hidden part of him, you are willing to forgive the way he behaves.

It can be intoxicating when the Bad Boy confides in you. On the first night you meet, he tells you that his father's death made him grow up faster. You're touched that he's showing you exactly who he is from the very start; he's fearless. Since most people wait to reveal intimate details about themselves and their histories, this immediate divulgence naturally leads you to think, "He's so honest with me; we must have a connection."

When Bad Boys make you feel uniquely close to them, you feel special just to be invited along for the ride. How flattering when the lone rebel wolf lets you into his world! You believe that even though he may have other people in his life, you are the only one who knows the *real* him. You feel privileged, and since you think you know his whole story, you're more likely to forgive him for small transgressions, like his refusal to speak to anyone at your family's Thanksgiving dinner or the time he borrowed your car and "forgot" to return it.

Sometimes your relationship translates into a mutual "us against the world" fantasy. You two are *simpatico,* made to understand each other (at least, you seem to understand him). This can suggest that he is there for you in the same unique way that you are there for him. It bonds you together like Bonnie and Clyde, and it also silences the concerned voices around you. Of course your family doesn't understand your Bad Boy; soon you're thinking that they've never understood you, either!

The man who gives you the illusion of unique closeness can be the most confusing of the Bad Boys, because in a sense your relationship with him mimics a healthy relationship; of course you want to feel uniquely close to your man! Nevertheless, it's a bad sign when what he reveals about himself is always meant to explain why he's letting you down.

Ask yourself the following questions before continuing with this relationship:

- Is he as interested in getting to know the "real you" as you are in him?
- Are you different when you are with him?
- Does he see how his past has affected his present and want to work on it?
- Does he see himself as "once a Bad Boy, always a Bad Boy," or is it just that he hasn't grown up yet?

Reason 3: He's Charismatic

The Bad Boy is unlike any other man you've ever known. He is confident, almost to the point of being cocky. He has a self-assuredness that other men try to acquire, a nonchalance and poise for which men's products and magazines profess to hold the secret. His sex appeal is hard to describe, but it's in the way he carries himself, the tone of his voice, the effortless way he commands a room—corny things you thought you'd never find yourself saying. His style and *charisma* are key elements to his sense of self.

All women who date men want one who is smart, confident, and passionate—so much so that it can be all too easy to overlook bad behavior in a man who is otherwise an extremely appealing person. These men are often so compelling and confident because of their achievements (both in the bedroom and out)—an intoxicating combination. When good qualities are used as an excuse for Bad Boy behavior, however, that's simply a Bad Boy in disguise.

Take, for example, a political activist who is so passionate about his cause or his candidate that he often forgets to call and tell you that he's running several hours (or days) late. When you complain about the wasted time and energy you've expended waiting for him, he becomes angry and insists that he's working to change the world.

Maybe he's a professor who's very intellectually deep but who has an awful lot of late-night meetings with graduate students and comes home smelling of perfume. Maybe he's a policeman who comes home from a hard day and wants to do nothing but drink beer and watch TV—only it seems that every day is a "hard day."

The Bad Boy is not just an unemployed dude on a motorcycle. He might deliver the mail, or he might deliver babies. He could be the man behind the counter at your local supermarket or the

> "Artie would smoke like a chimney, despite the fact that he knew it was not healthy. Always in his boots and jeans, he looked like a Levi's ad to me. He had a big dog named Mondo that he took everywhere with him. He laughed a little too loudly for my friends."

lawyer who gets you out of a traffic ticket. The main ingredient of the Bad Boy is charisma, combined with irresponsibility, and men with passion and intellect tend to have a lot of charisma. Charisma is the woman's Achilles' heel; most women melt under its compelling charms. Does he use his passion as an excuse for treating you badly? Does he always put you second (or third, fourth, or sixteenth)? The truth is that the Bad Boy may never reorganize his priorities.

Reason 4: He Seems Like a "Real" Man

A classic selling point of the Bad Boy is that he tends to be conventionally masculine.

You are wired to be attracted to a man who can protect you, and he definitely gives the impression that he could. Maybe he has street smarts and makes you feel safe the way no one else ever has. Maybe you know that he would go down swinging if a jerk at a bar insulted you, even if it meant that he got a broken nose. He may never actually fight, but he gives a great impression that he could and would if it became necessary. That may be exciting to you; nevertheless, the morning that you need his help to take your dog to the animal hospital, he oversleeps.

Some Bad Boys attach their behavior to athletic performance, either their own or that of others. No matter what's happening with you, your guy needs an entire week of isolation before his monthly Tae Kwon Do tournament. He pushed someone at a party for supporting the opposing team, and you had to break up the fight that ensued. In any case, sports are just an excuse for his poor behavior.

Some women enjoy a feeling of invincibility that is associated with feeling protected by their macho Bad Boy. He doesn't take any guff, and therefore you don't have to, either. You feel powerful, backed up, and supported—in theory. In practice, all that the macho bravado really means is that you will rarely, if ever, be more important to him than his friends, his sports team, and his bike are.

The prototypical "real man" Bad Boy can touch upon your most primal desire to be protected, and he can back this up with an attractive physical prowess. Women love the charismatic Bad Boys for their swagger and their spontaneity, but mostly women love the way that these men ooze masculinity. You feel safe, although given how self-centered he is, you might actually be the least safe you've ever been. This Bad Boy is a fantasy character who might not want to live in reality.

"My boyfriend dropped out of school to be a boxer. Although he did sort of look a little scruffy, he was a pretty low-key, quiet guy. I was attracted to the fact that he dreamed of being a pro fighter, but my family was all about academia."

Reason 5: He Is Different and Exciting

Because Bad Boys are defined by being different from your usual boyfriends, you may see his wild side as a breath of fresh air. Anything unfamiliar can have the glimmer of newness and excitement. If your family is totally into exercise, it might seem titillating to you that he spends Sundays napping on the couch. If your family never drank, it could be refreshing that he likes to have a few beers every night. If you would never say anything off-color to anyone, it might be a relief to be around a man who tells everyone, even strangers, exactly what's on his mind. Almost anything different from what you're used to can be fascinating.

For some women, the opportunity to be "bad" by association is secretly appealing. Women are brought up to be sweet and polite.

It's generally frowned upon for women to be too aggressive, outrageous, or irresponsible. This is good, to some degree, but it can also make it difficult to find a vicarious outlet for the shadier parts of one's personality.

All women have their dark sides—whether that means gossiping, indulging in recreational drugs, or worse—but few women freely express this side of themselves. A Bad Boy can therefore allow women to embrace their alter egos. Dating a man from the proverbial "wrong side of the tracks" has its allure, because women, too, get to live a little dangerously—without having to fully own it. This man encourages you to let your hair down, take it easy, and be irresponsible.

Other women seek a sort of adolescent rebellion. Since the Bad Boy usually runs counter to what those around you think is good for you, it feels rebellious to stand by him even as your friends and family present a laundry list of his faults. Maybe you've always wanted to be spontaneous, antagonistic, or irreverent but are unable to be those things because you fear the consequences. Along comes Mr. Bad Boy, and he's all too happy to live out your fantasies for you. However, instead of cultivating his best traits (like impulsiveness or spunk) in yourself, you're putting up with his worst qualities. For some women, this is easier than doing the hard work on themselves.

Finally, some women just find that Bad Boys are fun. Maybe it seems glamorous to ride around on his Harley or get really drunk on a Tuesday for no good reason. Perhaps his devil-may-care attitude is exactly what you need to jar yourself out of a personal or professional rut. Some women thrive on the passionate conflict that Bad Boys usually inspire. However, the party can last only so long.

The different and exciting Bad Boys are some of the most alluring because they bring a new element to your life, whether it's candor or partying. It's an easy way to try out a different way to live.

> "Tom was a classic Bad Boy. He played in a band, had tattoos, and had a different girlfriend every month. He picked fights and mocked rules. Sometimes it was fun for me to live vicariously on the wrong side of the tracks."

Ask yourself the following:

- Do you admire the things that make him different, or are they just seductive because you haven't experienced them before with a guy?
- Is he out of control with drugs or alcohol?
- Is his spontaneity affecting other parts of your life, like your job?

It's possible that he is in a "good times" phase of his life and will grow out of it—possible, but not likely.

The Good and Bad Sides of Life with a Bad Boy

The fact is that if the relationship was always awful, it would have been easier to walk away than to keep striving for change, but just as there were bad "lows," there must have been some really good "highs" that kept you there.

The good side: "He needs me." Some women seek their opposite in their Bad Boys: they thrive on feeling like a lighthouse of sanity and stability next to their out-of-control men. The guy goes on a weekend bender but shows up on Sunday night for some TLC. He gets arrested for fighting but calls you to bail him out. He calls you for rides, money, and a sympathetic ear. He obviously needs you, and that makes you feel better. Unfortunately, it also means that he may need you only to get him out of trouble. This means that you may unconsciously enjoy his escapades, for without them he might never call you.

Some Bad Boys rely on their girlfriends to rein in their more outrageous behavior. You can usually dissuade him from doing something destructive if you're around, such as by getting him home early on a night before an important meeting or talking him out of keying someone's car. If he's upset, you're there to calm him down. This is appealing because it gives you a sense of control over the situation; however, it's a tremendous and unfair responsibility.

At the other end of the spectrum is the Bad Boy who presents himself as a "broken man." He's really just a little boy with a hard exterior and a distaste for responsibility. It's not his fault that he's gruff or cynical—he's been jaded by circumstances. Maybe he was fired recently (or not so recently). Maybe he has low self-esteem because his mother didn't love him enough. The sweet soul deep inside him just needs some support to thrive.

The bottom line is that you enjoy feeling as if he is relying on you to get himself together; maybe it makes you feel as if you have your life together. This Bad Boy needs help, and you believe that you're the one to give it to him. You've always wanted to feel needed, maternal, and/or like a disciplinarian—but do you want a misbehaving teenage son or a boyfriend?

The bad side: His bad side makes you feel bad. He's unapologetic about who he is, even dismissive about your feelings. Some women are all too ready to think that they are the cause of problems in a relationship, and Bad Boys are always ready to nurture this impulse. These men never think that they are doing anything wrong. They're living by their own rules. So what that he's late to your birthday party? Lighten up! Yeah, he called your sister's husband a jerk! So what? You don't like him, either!

Eventually, his bad side starts to wear thin, producing the hallmark of the Bad Boy dynamic: you start to feel bad about yourself. You assume that you are repressed, prudish, or a nag. You are the one who is jealous, insecure, and a stick in the mud. All of a sudden you can't figure out how you have lost yourself. Instead of being more excited, you start to feel "not cool enough," repressed, and rigid. When his impulsiveness becomes old and you tell him that you want to be asked out ahead of time, he says that you lack spontaneity. When he cancels on you twice in one week and you ask him to stick to his word, he calls you a control freak.

These accusations can both directly and undeservedly deteriorate your self-worth. It's especially disorienting if you're hooked on him, because you know you cannot control whether he shows up for your date, so instead you focus on squelching your righteous anger. What is really crazy is that you end up feeling selfish when you demand better treatment.

These situations are some of the most destructive in the Bad Boy scenario. If friends and family try to intervene, they, too, become the objects of his criticism. He says that your sister, who called him a deadbeat, is such a snob. Your parents don't like him because he's a "freethinker." This allows him to openly disregard anything that you or those close to you have to say about his behavior. Stop, take a deep breath, and before you start blaming yourself, answer the following questions:

- Does he take your complaints seriously?
- Does he bad-mouth your friends or family?
- All relationships involve compromise; can he handle it?

The answers should tell you if he is a Bad Boy in need of your help or simply Bad News.

How to Know If Your "Bad" Bad Boy Can Become a "Good" Bad Boy

You don't want him to become a spineless mama's boy, but curbing that really bad behavior would make life so much easier. You may want edgy but appropriate when the situation calls for it, even the occasional streak of irreverence that electrifies a conversation, but here the key words are *appropriate* and *occasional.*

1. *Look at him.* Some of the traits listed previously sound familiar to you, but you're not convinced that your man is really a Bad Boy. He has stood you up many times. He got wasted at your friend's cocktail party and called your sister a slut—on Christmas, yet. Nevertheless, you're not convinced that he's a Bad-to-the-Bone Bad Boy.

   Examine your Bad Boy closely—put him under the microscope. Is there an actual, *temporary* reason that he's so rough around the edges, defiant, and unpredictable? Did his mother just die? Is he traveling frequently for a new job? Is he working on some big, important project such as a benefit for homeless children? These things would probably result in some typical Bad Boy behavior, but it would pass with time.

   Sometimes men act with extra bravado in the early stages of a relationship to cover for a whole host of normal feelings, like anxiety and insecurity. Is it possible that he's just trying to impress you and that he'll calm down as soon as he feels more comfortable? Is his bravado just an act? It's possible, in the early stages of dating, for Bad Boy traits to manifest themselves for other reasons.

2. *Look at yourself.* The best way to know if you are with a Bad Boy is to see how *you* end up feeling or behaving. Many times, a "relationship" with a Bad Boy (if that's what you want to call it) is a roller coaster of emotions. You're way up high when he gives you attention, then low, low, low when he disappoints you. You become addicted to this back-and-forth because it holds your interest. He gets your

blood pumping and your adrenaline gushing; it's easy to mistake all the energy and bouts of tears for hot-blooded passion.

Be on the lookout for poor decisions that are influenced by your Bad Boy. Do you say yes to things you would never have agreed to in the past, just because it means spending time with your guy? Whether you stay out late on a work night or agree to play paintball with him in your stilettos, the general underlying theme is that you give up a piece of yourself in order to keep him around. Maybe you're happy to do things he enjoys, but he would never consider staying home with you on a Friday night to watch movies, which you enjoy. Relationships are always a give-and-take, but does it seem as though you give a lot more than you get to take?

3. *Look to your friends*. Although your friends are usually good barometers for how awful your boyfriends are, it may be hard to hear what they are trying to tell you. Sometimes they don't come out and just say what they mean. Maybe they merely hint that your Bad Boy is beneath you. Maybe they gently ask why you keep seeking and going out with the exact same type of guy over and over. If you're lucky, your friends will just outright call your Bad Boy a loser or a thug to your face; if you're not so lucky, they'll say it behind your back. If your guy is rough around the edges (or pretends to be), a few people have probably raised an eyebrow or asked straight out what you see in him.

   The trick here is not to reject what your friends say. You certainly can't take everyone's advice unreservedly, but you can pick the friends whom you trust the most and solicit feedback from them. Ask the ones you feel closest to if anything concerns them about your boyfriend. As outsiders, they may see things differently and be able to offer objective advice when you are too deeply involved to see clearly. (Of course, if you have to ask, then you already know the answer.)

Be on guard: sometimes you will "translate" your friends' words (see the table below) in your mind as you try to excuse your Bad Boy's egregious behavior.

They Say He Is	You See Him As
Crass	Honest
Obnoxious	Defiant
Drunk	Fun
Disturbed	Misunderstood
Angry	Passionate
In need of psychiatric help	Unconditionally in love with you
Immature	Boyish
Moody	Sensitive
Flirtatious	Sensual
Irresponsible	Living in the moment
Unfaithful	Free-spirited

Why Do Women Tolerate Bad Behavior?

At a certain point, women have to look at their options. If the Bad Boy is bad for them, then who is the "good guy" and why don't they want him? If he's the opposite of the Bad Boy, then he would be thoughtful, secure, and honest. It sounds great, doesn't it? Nevertheless, how often have you heard a friend say that she rejected a man because he was "too nice"? Women miss those Bad Boy traits: overt masculinity, spontaneity, rebelliousness. It might not make sense, but it seems that women are programmed to be susceptible to the Bad Boys of the world.

Does This Sound Like Your Man?

incorrigible *adj* 1: impossible to correct or reform 2: very difficult to control or keep in order

At the heart of the Bad Boy's appeal is your belief that he will change. The fear that keeps you with him is that if he doesn't alter himself for you, he will do so for the next woman waiting in the wings, and you will have just missed this great reformed Bad Boy. Face it, women want it all: the sexy rebel *and* the reliable boyfriend. Women tell themselves to be patient, that he'll come around sooner or later and be oh-so appreciative of how she helped him to become a better person. This is a fantasy, but it sustains most women through a Bad Boy relationship.

The Tucker Max Syndrome

You may not have heard of him, but Tucker Max is a self-made Bad Boy poster dude. He's proud to report on his Web site that he likes to "get excessively drunk at inappropriate times, disregard social norms, indulge every whim, mock idiots and posers, sleep with more women than is safe or reasonable, and just generally act like a raging d–head."

Not only do people eat up the details of his escapades on his blog, he seems to have no trouble getting women to go to bed with him. How is this possible? He's the prototypical twenty-first-century Bad Boy—unapologetically putting himself out there for everyone to see, and some poor misguided woman out there thinks that she's going to reform this guy.

The Bad Boy Solution

Unless you really enjoy riding an emotional roller coaster, you are going to have to do some soul-searching to figure out what your Bad Boy can do, what you can do, and what will never happen with this man. The only time you can convince him to settle down is when he's already halfway there (more about this in chapter 7).

Let's assume he's at the "I am what I am" stage of life (which usually goes with "I never planned on living past thirty, anyway"). If you're looking to get a grip on your relationship with your Bad Boy, start by writing some things down. It can be difficult in the heat of the moment of confrontation to remember your most important points. Maybe you say that he's always late and he says that he's not, but if you have a list of specific instances, then neither of you can fudge the facts. Make your list and then examine your own expectations. Are you living in a fantasy world? Women who are into Bad Boys tend to develop an attachment to romantic notions that might not stand up in reality.

Of course, you don't want your Bad Boy to morph into some spineless sitcom husband, but your fantasy is that you could tame him just enough. You would love him for exactly the Bad Boy he is; you only want him to recognize that you are, in fact, the woman for him and that therefore he should modify his behavior slightly in order to be with you. Therein lies the catch-22. A Bad Boy lives by his own rules, and these rules (or lack thereof) are what attracted you to him in the first place.

What it comes down to is that Bad Boys never see their behavior as wrong, thoughtless, or just plain bad. They are simply doing their own thing in the world, and they can't understand why you don't adjust to them. The Bad Boy never pretended to be anything else. He is exactly what he showed you in the beginning, and that's how he'll stay, so ask yourself, "Even if his bad boyishness is attractive now, how will it look on him in ten or twenty years?"

Some women are so attracted to their Bad Boys that they keep reinforcing the men's behavior, such as by calling in sick for them when they're too hung over to dial the phone or by simply waiting around for them to show up. Even if you're not consciously applauding the choices your Bad Boy makes, it's unlikely that he'll learn to be different, because there will always be a woman in the wings with a weakness for him.

Is the Bad Boy a fixer-upper? Relationship reform schools rarely end in the woman's favor. Although the occasional Bad Boy may change, most will always be as they were when you found them.

Such a man might get to the point where he openly tells you that he loves you, that you are nothing like anyone he's ever had before, but scars from his past rugged exterior and defiant attitude tell another story. Keep in mind the following:

- Rather than picking a Bad Boy and trying to discourage his bad qualities, pick a good boy who has a hint of Bad Boy qualities.
- Keep notes of what he promised.
- Watch yourself for blanket statements that other men are "boring."
- Be aware of the fact that the longer you wait for him to grow up, the more time you'll waste.
- Never forget that dating should be fun and easy, not a full-time job.

6

Refine Your Target

For a man, the ideal woman will never nag. She'll find his quirks and downfalls endearing, or she'll weigh the good and the bad and decide to leave well enough alone because the good is very good. Whether a guy drinks straight out of the milk carton or is never on time for anything, this forgiving mythical woman will either shrug (preferably with a smile) or somehow compensate for it, becoming the part that "completes" him as she signs his name to thank-you cards and sends birthday gifts to his mom from him every year.

This, of course, is not only absolute nonsense, it's a complete fantasy. The woman described above is either a well-paid personal assistant or a doting, demented grandmother.

Relationships are hard work. Not only are women a different sex—which means that their brains are wired differently—they're also raised differently, listen differently, and have different expectations and goals. It's actually a small miracle that men and women have anything in common. Lust or chemistry brings them together, then daily life and the reality of how hard it is to negotiate and understand each other (over the years) makes the relationship extremely challenging. Women and men are practically aliens from different planets and different galaxies who don't share a common language, yet they have to put together an Ikea bed with instructions badly translated from Swedish.

"Why doesn't she just accept me the way I am?" a man keeps thinking. "She met me like this, and I haven't changed. *She* has changed." You, in contrast, keep asking yourself why he won't change—or at least just change a few small (to him) but important (to you) habits. After all, you give in all the time in disagreements. He wants the air conditioning in the car set higher, so you point all the vents at him. Why can't he at least put the cap on the toothpaste, then? Both actions take two seconds and half a calorie to do. You find yourself becoming frustrated and angry. "He knows how much it bothers me, so why won't he just stop?" you find yourself screaming in your head.

You take on the challenge. You just can't let it go; it has become personal. You decide that you will teach him through logic, trick him, or use dog-training techniques. This is not just some whim of yours; it will be good for him to change—and not just to please you, but to be a better person himself, to be an adult. Your motives are unquestionable. You set the goals: to stop him from biting his nails, to stop him from staring at cleavage, to persuade him to elevate his career aspirations, or to wean him from eating so much heart-clogging trans fat. Although you are doing it for yourself, it is really mostly for him.

Stop right there and take a deep breath. Before you decide that you will teach him, trick him, or dog-train him to make him pay attention, you need to do some good hard thinking and determine *exactly* what has to change. You have to start by *defining* the objective behavior or trait, really whittling the bothersome quality down to the most specific description possible. What are the circumstances in which it happens? What is he thinking (if anything) at the time? What are the variations and range of the activity?

Specificity is the name of the game. How precisely can you pinpoint your target behavior? Blanket statements like "he's a slob" or "he is close-minded" may be true, but we want to figure out the *precise and specific* action that drives you crazy. Maybe it's a characteristic or an activity that you'd like to extinguish completely—no lying, no smoking, no picking his nose—or maybe you just want him to learn not to do it in front of you, ever.

Be Specific

Unraveling a blanket descriptor that only indicates your frustration lets you zero in on one habit and take it apart, thread by thread. Let's start with an example.

Complaint: "Jerry has terrible hygiene; he's just a stinky mess." Now be *specific*.

Q He doesn't brush his teeth *ever*? What exactly do you mean by *hygiene*? And what is *stinky*? Does he smell bad?

A Oh, he brushes his teeth and uses soap when he showers; it's just that he doesn't change his clothes. I mean, he'll wear them over and over, and it's gross. They smell, and since he's wearing them, he smells. But he doesn't seem to notice!

Q So his underwear and his socks smell, or is it his jeans?

A His gym clothes. He'll wear the same sweatpants five days in a row.

Q Why? What is he thinking?

A Oh, he figures, why wash them when he is just going to sweat in them the next day. He figures he'll wear a clean pair once a week, even though I've bought him four or five pairs of new ones.

The problem is now better defined, from "he has terrible hygiene" to "he wears the same sweatpants to the gym five days in a row." This is certainly a simplistic example, but it gets you out of the "Why, why, why?" stage, stops your internal muttering, relieves your frustration, and gives you something to hold on to—a plan of action. So take that ICK and break it down with surgical precision, zero in on *why* it bothers you, and then ask yourself these questions:

1. If you didn't have to see it, if he did it when you weren't around, would that make things more tolerable?
2. Is the fact that he does it in front of other people part of the reason that it drives you crazy?
3. Do you believe that he represents you as a couple and that this behavior makes you look "bad"?
4. Does it bother you that he continues with the same bothersome habit even though you have given him a simple solution?

5. Is what makes you crazy the fact that this quirk is so discrepant with the rest of his personality?
6. Is there a "gross factor" involved (something to do with germs, something nasty or unpleasant)?

The next step is to narrow down your blanket statement to the most precise definition by taking it apart, strand by strand.

The complaint: He's always late.

Q Do you care if he's late to his meetings?

A No, it bothers me only when he is supposed to do something with me and I am left waiting for him.

Q Is it the idea that he is not punctual that bothers you or the fact that you are stuck without anything to do until he arrives?

A Actually, what bothers me is that I am losing time when I could be doing something else. If he's late and I'm working at home, it doesn't bother me nearly as much as when I'm waiting for him at a restaurant.

Q Is he late because his meetings run over, or is he distracted by something and doesn't leave at the right time? Is it something he controls, or does someone else control it?

Do this back-and-forth questioning until you get to the heart of the problem, the nitty-gritty. Which particulars can you

"While I was working on being more specific about what bothers me, I realized that I was describing the very things I said I liked about him when I met him. Gordon was so romantic, so free-spirited, and such an independent thinker. Now I am frustrated with him because he can't seem to keep his feet on the ground; he's so unrealistic. I felt crazy when I realized this. Can't I have a little of that free, crazy guy but also have some stability?"

live with, and which ones make you want to bite his head off (which brings out a side of you that you don't like and never even knew you had)?

Assess His Moldability Potential

Whatever the issue is, it's important to home in on the particular characteristic that is driving you up the wall, because once you do, you can move on to part two of the process by asking some key questions: Is there potential for change, or will you grow old together with you repeating the same thing over and over until your last breath? Is there potential for change, but you just haven't figured out how to present it in order to get through to him? Is there, in fact, *zero* potential that you or anyone will persuade him to change? If the latter is the case, everyone should just back off and leave him alone—but at least you know.

Nothing in life is easy, but some things tend to be easier than others. Determining the specifics of what you want to change will give you the tools you need in order to assess his moldability potential and, consequently, the possibility of success. With our process, you can find out whether you need elbow grease or something short of a miracle to make him change his ways. So, before you waste your time, let's get started.

Open the Box: Bad Habit or Personality Flaw?

What do you wish he would change? Not every problem presents the same degree of difficulty. By asking yourself the following questions, you'll be starting to weed out the impossible and focus on the possible.

1. Is it
   a. A characteristic intrinsic to his personality, such as laughing when he is nervous?

   b. A bad habit, such as not picking up his dirty laundry from the floor?

2. Is it
   a. Something that has started recently, such as getting a new job that requires his spending weekends working?
   b. Something he has always been accused of, such as having poor social skills in group settings as far back as not sharing his toys in kindergarten?

3. Is it
   a. Something he does out of habit, such as using a big dollop of hair gel when the bottle clearly says "pea-size amount" on the label?
   b. A trait that he thinks is integral to his identity, such as being cynical and sarcastic because he's a philosophy major?

4. Is it
   a. Something that should change with age?
   b. Something that no matter how old or mature he becomes, he'll take to the grave?

As you read and think about your answers, write down and seriously acknowledge your first reaction, not what happens when you think it through and decide that you might even change your mind the second time. It should be an automatic, knee-jerk reaction—the way things look right now, not where you hope he'll be next year or what the ICK is like once you help him to understand something.

You should also definitely include his take on the situation. However, if he is thirty-five and continues to wear baby blue and howl "Duke sucks" throughout March Madness, it's possible that his sports fanaticism could change with age, but it's also possible that it has become a core personality trait.

It shouldn't come as a surprise to you to discover that personality traits like laziness and moodiness will be harder to amend than

Realization One-Timers

The most satisfying of all ICKs are the ones that once you point them out, he'll look surprised and change immediately. "Oh, that little fork on the end is the salad fork? Thanks, I didn't know that." "The correct pronunciation of *comparable* is to put the accent on the first syllable? Thanks for telling me." "The standard tip in Manhattan for a cab is 15 percent? Got it!"

Sometimes he won't even make a big deal of it, or he'll brush it off by saying, "Oh well, now I know." The only time you'll find resistance is when he says that the new way seems "chumpy" and that the group he thinks he'd be "joining" are suckers.

habits like holding his fork in a full-fisted grip. Breaking a habit is much easier than rewiring the frontal cortex. That doesn't mean it's out of the question, however. There are many variables that exist in any situation, and this is no different.

If you date an actor and his constant need to be the center of attention irritates you to no end, then you have a difficult road ahead of you. There are no absolutes, but it is very likely that if you date an entertainer, he will continue to entertain—and it will probably be with monologues. Will the nitpicking accountant be able to relax at home and not organize the spice rack by size and color?

Before you proceed any further, start with a few basic questions. Consider them with complete honesty, without adding what you think he could do or what you are wishing for him to do. As hard as it is, answer the following questions truthfully. No one is listening to or judging what you are thinking:

- Can he change for you?
- Will he change for you?

- What could you do to be less irritated?
- Can you do something to get him halfway there, enabling him to go the rest of the way on his own?

These are things we'll talk more about in the next chapter, but we want you to start to think about them now. We are going to attack this problem from all angles and find a solution, maybe even a creative one, by really understanding where the weak link is and how to do enough tweaking for life to be manageable with him (or for you to realize that it is never going to happen and to stop wasting your time).

We've already pointed out that there is a fundamental difference between wrestling with an attribute that has always been indicative of who he is versus a habit that has developed more recently. You must take into account whether he is responding to a situation or is just being the same person he has always been. For example, has he always been frugal, or is he worrying more about money since the stock market took a hit?

If the characteristic in question is part of his self-identity, then change won't come easy. Now examine his motivation. Is the trait in question something that you alone want him to change, or is it something that he wants to change for himself? Does he actually acknowledge that it is a bad habit? If the incentive lies within him, then the possibility for success is exponentially greater.

Do the Math

In order to assess his moldability, read the following four sets of questions and answer "high" or "low," depending on your personal scenario. Keep in mind that these are subjective; don't judge how important they are to the world at large. If something bothers you, remember that that is why you are about to create a moldability profile.

Be ruthless in your assessment: it's not how you would like life to be, it's what is right in front of you, plain as day. (If you need help being realistic, have your best girlfriend answer for you, then discuss it if necessary. (Don't try to convince her or yourself otherwise, or you'll confuse the scoring.)

1. *You.* How much of a role do *you* play in his motivation to change? Does he want to please you? Is he afraid that you may finally decide that the ICK is a deal breaker and walk away? Does he have a pattern of changing or adjusting things simply to make you happy? How about when you've become angry and eyed the door? Is your love the leverage?
2. *The environment.* How much environmental support can you draw from in order to make the change? Are his friends, coworkers, or family going to make it harder for him to stop or behave differently? Will they make fun of him, tempting him to go back to his old behavior, or will they support him in not smoking, gambling, or engaging in other bad behavior?
3. *Control.* How much can he control the behavior now? Is it a habit he can change fairly easily, or is it something he'd really have to push himself to change? (Make sure to think about this from *his* perspective, not yours.)
4. *Himself.* How important is the change for him personally? That is, without you in the picture, would he still want to work on it, or would he breathe a sigh of relief and go back to his old ways? Change will be a lot easier if the motivation for it lies within him.

Scoring

High, High, High, High. Congratulations! There's a good chance that with a little TLC, you could end up with the man of your dreams. Not only does he want to improve for you, he wants to do it for himself. He has support (or at least no interference) from the outside world, and what you are asking him to do is not that hard for him. In fact, in the time it's taken you to read this chapter, he has probably gone and done it already.

This is a man who just had to be given a suggestion, a slight nudge. He was simply waiting for someone to come along and take him shopping for new clothes or introduce him to nose-hair clippers.

High, High, High, Low. He'd do pretty much anything to make you smile (or to have you stop crying), his family would be there to provide the backup that he needs, and making the change won't take much blood, sweat, and tears. There is one integral person in the way, however: himself. Here we have a man who wants to do it for you, who has the people in his life supporting his efforts, and who has the ability to transform, but he just doesn't want it for himself.

He won't pick his teeth when you are around, but the second you are out of the room he'll be reaching for a business card or a frayed toothpick. Do you need for him to want the change for himself, or are you okay with the fact that he'll never grasp why this is critical for him? Whether it's going to church on Sunday or eating fruit and vegetables for a healthy colon, he really, really doesn't care about it at all and probably never will. Are you okay with that, as long as he just *does* it?

High, High, Low, High. Although this guy has a long uphill climb ahead of him, he is lucky to have all the backing he needs to make the transformation. Maybe he wants to stop drinking and his family wants that, too, and he wants to make you happy with him—but, gosh darn it, those twelve steps are really steep. Maybe you want him to learn Spanish so that you can move back to Spain, or maybe you want him to have therapy for his fear of flying; these are hard changes to make. The good news is that he has the support to do it and he wants to do it for himself as well as for you.

High, Low, High, High. If his friends and coworkers continue to be bad influences, the situation is tricky but not dire. His own desire and your devotion to the cause could very well prevail over the others in his life. The fact that he is able to control the ICK, that it's not so difficult to change, may ultimately allow him to succeed. Maybe he was addicted to nicotine, but since a severe asthma attack last year he has been able to kick smoking with little trouble—until he goes out with his friends, who smoke in front of him. Maybe his friends will tempt him with a line of cocaine. Regardless of what the vice is, just keeping him away from these bad influences and reinforcing your policing efforts will not work. What you have going for you is that your ICK is specific to a time and a place.

Low, High, High, High. Although it may initially feel like a blow that he doesn't think he should change for you, the reality is that he wants to change for himself, and there is no greater motivation than this.

Low, Low, High, High. It will be harder for him to change without the support of the people in his life. The fact that he is not changing in order to please you doesn't mean that he won't be able to beat the odds. If it's easy enough, and he wants it badly enough, he can do it with you supporting him.

Low, High, Low, High. Change will take a serious effort on his part. In this case, it's best that you exercise patience, but with the environmental factors on his side, he has a relatively high moldability profile.

Low, High, High, Low. If he doesn't care enough about making the change for himself, *and* he's not doing it to please you, then the only motivator is society or his family. The saving grace here is that he has good control over the ICK, so there is a possibility, however slight, that he will make adjustments for the other people in his life.

High, Low, Low, High. If he really wants to change the thing that is driving you crazy, then you are dealing with a higher-than-average moldability profile. The negative here is that he will have a hard time breaking the habit and maintaining the good behavior in light of the lack of support from those around him. In fact, they might even pull him back in, saying that he's henpecked.

High, Low, High, Low. He wants to do it for you, but if you weren't there, he wouldn't think twice about it. In this case, although it may seem easy enough to get rid of the ICK, the motivating factor will mostly reside with you. This is tricky, because the threat of losing you has to be strong enough on its own to kick him into gear.

High, High, Low, Low. It's hard for him to kick the habit, and although he is surrounded by people who have his back, he is not champing at the bit to be made over. Since the main reason he's doing it is for everyone else except himself, the potential for change is less than likely.

Low, Low, Low, Low. With absolutely no motivator and little control, there is no reason to think that there is any change in sight.

High, Low, Low, Low. If the only reason he wants to change is for you, it could happen, but only very slowly over time. More than likely, there will be many false starts along the way or the ICK will change only temporarily.

Low, High, Low, Low. He's not interested in stopping the behavior simply because it makes you angry, and he's not interested in changing for himself, because he likes himself the way he is. His family agrees. Ultimatums from you only make *you* look crazy, so the only recourse may be to curb the undesirable behavior in certain situations. Even then you are left being bad cop—not a fun job.

Low, Low, High, Low. Change is easy here—mind-numbingly easy. However, he doesn't care what you think, he doesn't care what his friends and family think, and he doesn't feel like changing. Doing it halfway for him might be the key here, or change might be triggered by a tragic event.

Low, Low, Low, High. Since the motivation to change lies with him, the chances for change are very good. It may take hard work and determination, but if he's unwavering, he can do it. Others' reactions, including yours, make no difference in his choice of action.

Why, Exactly, Do You Want Him to Change?

Throughout a relationship, the woman is running a series of unconscious but specific calculations on the man in question. A deal-breaker form of behavior (discussed below) will, of course, terminate the analysis and the relationship. However, if he is strong in some categories that are important to the woman—such as emotional and financial stability, good looks, and kindness—she will overlook flaws in height, wit, or style.

Some of these shortcomings are at the top of your "things to change in him" list. This is often well intentioned; you want him to be the best and happiest version of himself that he can be.

Sometimes your motivations are not entirely altruistic and have more to do with the opinions of your friends and family. As we pointed out before, most women with this sort of list tell themselves that this project is genuinely altruistic, because if he fixed these problems he'd be better off—and sometimes that's true. Thus it's essential that you determine what's at the root of your request.

If there were a mathematical equation for how women choose and deal with their boyfriends' shortcomings, it would have to take into account hundreds of variables and unknowns. Here are some big ones; these are the questions you should ask yourself in order to zero in on the part you play in the issue with your man:

- Did he do this behavior when you first met him? That is, has he always been this way, but lately it has started to bother you more? Are you really annoyed about something else and displacing your anger?
- Is his behavior something that doesn't bother anyone but you? Is it just an inane pet peeve of yours (but you don't have many, and everyone has at least one that is inexplicably weird)? Does he have a pet peeve about you, and have you given in about it? Are you digging in your heels because it has a personal or historical meaning for you?
- Is his behavior a sign of pure disrespect for you? Does he take the relationship for granted, or does his quirk feel that way to you? Does the way he treats you truly show disrespect, and, more important, is this just the tip of the iceberg? (Beware—it might be!)
- Is this behavior something he promised would change, something you hoped he'd grow out of, or something you hoped would bother you less as the two of you grew closer?

If so, why are you hanging in there? What is keeping you tethered?

- Is his behavior something that is driving you apart, that is destructive to your relationship, to your children, or to your respective families? Is it a very big issue like jealousy, truth, or safety (which is maybe rearing its head as a small thing, but your gut knows it's about something larger)? If it is so serious, how much calm face-to-face discussion time have you dedicated to it?
- Are you embarrassed by his ICK for yourself, are you worried for him, or are you worried about how others see him? How much does he worry? Why doesn't he worry more?
- This process is about growing. Is his behavior something that all adults should know, or is it something that would make him a more well-rounded person? Is his inflexibility driving you crazy, or is it the retort that "I am just fine the way I am and don't want to consider any new information"?
- Is his behavior something that he has tried to change before? Is it something that other girlfriends have tried to change in him? Does he understand the steps he has to take to effect change, or does he see the whole thing as an overwhelming and impossible challenge?
- Is his behavior encouraged, tolerated, or enabled by his environment (for example, he plays sports

"When determining why the things I had listed about him made me so mad, I realized that they in themselves weren't heinous things (the cap off the toothpaste, the sponge facedown in the sink), and it was too much to go through such a fight every time. I had to realize that there were things he did really well and did just for me. I could continue to remind him and get in a huff, or I could take half a second, sigh, and let it roll off me and try not to sweat the small stuff."

with his buddies, most of his social life revolves around sports, and even his business dealings involve playing a sport with clients)?

- Is his behavior something that he thinks is your problem and not his (for example, you are "oversensitive")?

Answering these questions should start giving you a game plan. You should now have an idea of how rooted the ICK is in his personality, how deeply ingrained it is in his patterns of behavior. You should understand why it bothers you and where the irritation comes from. Most important, you should have a notion of how changeable the behavior is and what is an acceptable response or amount of change from him in order for you to stay in the relationship and be content.

The Thing You Loved May Be the Thing You Come to Hate

You may be surprised to hear that a patient often uncovers in therapy that her gripe with her man is over the very same thing that initially attracted her to him. This may sound counterintuitive. Women's emotions are hardwired to push them into long-term romantic relationships (or at least enough to have children); but sometimes there are short circuits, and you are attracted to qualities that will ultimately repel you. Does this sound familiar?

Then: "He was so romantic when we met in a bar; he asked me if I had seen Jupiter that night."

Now: "He has his head in the clouds; I can't get him to be realistic about a job or a career."

Then: "He was so spontaneous. He just would show up at my place with flowers or a homemade pie."

Now: "It's impossible to make plans with this guy, even for big events."

Before we proceed to the next chapter, you should clarify a few more points about why he is not doing what you want. Circle the numbers of the ones that you think pertain to you.

1. He doesn't realize how much it upsets me. (That is, I am not making it clear to him that this is something that, on a scale of one to ten, is a nine.)
2. He realizes how much it upsets me, but it seems illogical to him, so he won't change it. I think he knows that it makes me want to scream, but he figures that he won't give in to something that makes so little sense to him. "What is the big deal? Chill out, babe," he says. In fact, the moment he senses that I am bringing up "that topic," his eyes automatically glaze over, he has a narcoleptic attack, or he becomes so exasperated that he just walks away.
3. He is too lazy to change. It's too much of an effort for him to stand up, walk to the kitchen, and put his glass in the sink. He doesn't care if the glass stays on the coffee table. If I care so much, he believes, then I should pick it up. Whatever it is that I want him to do takes a huge amount of effort, and he can't really tell me why. Doing bicep curls with forty-pound weights is fun, but taking a four-pound bag of garbage out is not. He'll even admit that he's lazy—is that supposed to make me feel better?
4. He figures that because I do things that bother him and he doesn't bug me about it, I should be able to put up with his bits and pieces. (This man-math works only if you have agreed on it together; then it's called a *compromise*. It's the "you wash, I'll dry" scenario.) He has decided on his own, for instance, that his love of electronics equals my love of kitchen appliances. He wants to buy a coin organizer that

some gadget magazine says is a 2010 must-have; does this compare to the toaster oven I had to replace when the one that was a wedding present finally died? His gadget du jour usually lasts for a few days, whereas a new toaster oven will be making toast for the whole family for the next ten years. Why can't he see the difference?

5. It's really hard to break the habit. He's been doing it that way for ten, twenty, or thirty years. He thinks that since I don't have this habit, I have no sensitivity about how hard it is to break. ("Babe, you're so healthy and straitlaced you don't even drink caffeinated tea! Nicotine is harder than heroin! Cut me some slack.")

6. He figures that if he changes this one thing, the list will continue to grow until he's just an automaton who does everything I say. "Yeah, you know what happens then," his buddy says to him. "Yup, brother, I know," he answers. "That 'one little thing and you'd be perfect' somehow becomes two things, then three, then four, and all of a sudden I have a whole laundry list of 'little things.'"

   "Or," his buddy adds, "as soon as one is done, another one is added, so you always have one. It's what hell is, I think. As soon as you take the garbage out, you come back and there is another full bag, and it's always leaking. And she's always squawking that it wouldn't be leaking if you'd done it sooner. There's no out, my friend. Want another beer?"

> "When I was growing up, my mom prided herself on training my dad in everything. She'd brag how she had broken him of his bad habits. The house was hers, and it ran like clockwork. To him, however, a successful family was one in which there was flexibility. People complemented each other. It wasn't about winning a battle."

Does he keep giving you the impression that he will do what you want, and then you become increasingly heated because he doesn't do it? What gives you the impression that he's amenable? His not listening starts to feel disrespectful. The issue moves from being a mere annoyance to being a point of respect for you. When he sees his reaction to your request, does the fear grow in you that maybe you made a mistake and he is not the man you should be with?

7

Change Him, Mold Him

Given what you have read, assessed, and specifically defined so far, you have come to the conclusion—solid or wavering—that your man might be able to change. Here's your opportunity to bring out his potential or, on the other hand, your chance to finally become fed up, be pushed over the edge, develop the gumption to tip the scales, and move on.

In this chapter, we will show you the best way to approach the situation. We will give you the tools you need to determine how to bring up the issue diplomatically, slip it in subliminally, or erase the fantasy from your brain.

Perhaps you just haven't described your dissatisfaction in terms that were clear enough for him to understand. This approach might enable him to budge an inch, and that's all that's necessary, or else he won't budge at all. Then you know the deal; so, if necessary, you can throw up your hands, say "no más," pack your bags, and never have to put the toilet seat down again. Any solution is better than what you've been doing: sitting and waiting and hoping. Life is short, so let's get moving.

Change: A Dirty Word or a Life Process?

Everyone is a work in progress; everyone is in the process of evolving, whether it's by learning from one's own mistakes or from the experiences of those who are wiser. Many men may agree in theory, but the actual practice of taking in information, considering opinions, and reinventing themselves seems like conceding defeat or admitting that they aren't as good as they think they are.

Women, in contrast, are so used to assessing physiological and emotional changes throughout their lives that they tend to be more flexible and open to change. Women ask for opinions more often—sometimes too many times.

In dating, events become magnified and complicated, so the whole situation can become very touchy. You may think, "If I did something that was as unattractive and unpleasant as what he does, I'd want him to tell me!" That's probably true, because you are a female. Women ask for feedback. Women want to know how a new sweater fits, if the new cut really favors them, if people like them, if they're being understood. Women are neurologically wired and culturally trained to be solicitous of and responsive to feedback.

For men, asking for criticism (constructive or otherwise) and then reaching a compromise can make them feel bad rather than good. A man who changes the way he dresses for a woman might secretly think, "This means that I am not firm in my sense of self. I am wishy-washy, even spineless."

Understanding His Reaction to Change

Even the most agreeable man may cringe at the slightest indication that he is being thought of as a project. "You don't like me as I am?" he might think. That's just the point, however: you *do* like him for who he is—a lot. Nevertheless, you also love him for who he is capable of becoming. You recognize his heart of gold and you love the sound of his infectious laugh, but you acknowledge that there are still a few things to tweak. For example, you don't like one of his friends, he smokes too much pot, or you will never be okay with him not wearing socks with sneakers.

Usually you tiptoe around these issues because you fear that he will think you are shallow or that he will say something like "What's the big deal that I watch a little porn? Every guy does. I'm not changing. If you can't deal with it, then find someone else." Of course, men would never communicate that clearly. Honestly, women would appreciate a guy who could say, "Look, I'm never, never going to cover my mouth when I sneeze—not this week, not this year, not in ten years. I'll turn to one side, but that's it. That is the truth. So if you want to be with me, learn to deal with it, or find another guy." That's *our* ideal response. More likely, he'll say something similar to the following:

- "That was a small sneeze; it doesn't count."
- "I always cover my mouth; you just caught the rare one when I didn't."

- "What sneeze?"
- "I have ultrafast sneezes, and I can't get my hand to my mouth in time. Doctors are amazed. I know, it's nuts!"
- "Sure, doll. Pass me the salt."

Depending on the extent of change you want and whether he feels manipulated, this is where the games begin. Let's start by breaking down his reaction to your wanting him to do something differently. He could be thinking the following:

- "If I do this, there will be a hundred other changes coming down the pike at me. If I give in, the list of changes will never end. It's the tipping point; I can't give in."
- "If I do what she wants, it's pretty much like telling her that she has the control in this relationship. I might as well hand her a leash."

Unfortunately, these thought patterns tend to be unconscious, so you can't just say, "Hey, it's really only these two things that I want changed, and I'll be happy. Really, I don't want to put you on a leash!" He won't know what you are talking about.

Relationship Diplomacy

You're with a man who has a flaw that you want to adjust, and it's time to communicate the problem, explain your rationale, and offer a solution. This is a crucial step, and unfortunately it has no one-size-fits-all solution. To make sure that your game plan has the possibility of succeeding and doesn't backfire in your face, take time to ask yourself the following questions:

- How does he react to change in general, especially constructive criticism?
- Does he feel pressured when you ask him for feedback?

- At what times does he hear things the best?
- At what times does he seem most resistant to your suggestions and start to set up roadblocks?
- Have you observed any tactics that his friends and family use that actually work to make him listen without feeling irritated?

After you've taken the time to answer these questions, you have to determine whether it is worthwhile to attempt a renovation. You have to establish how plausible the change actually is and what is the most effective way to encourage the alteration you wish to see. Focus once again on the multiple factors that determine the potential paths to a solution.

Negotiating

You've grappled with your issues, then made your game plan and presented it to your mate. He is aware of the problems and has shown some resistance, either in word or in deed, to the proposed changes. Be aware: this phase of the relationship can be plagued by some common emotional fireworks. At this point, you need to break down the Big Issue into particulars. You've done this before, but it still needs to be refined:

- Is this irritant something that you could live with if it were minimized? Name three practical ways that this could happen.
- Does he understand how truly annoying his behavior is and why you want him to change it?
- Does he really understand the actual thing you want him to change—not the vague phrase that sounds like building an addition onto the house or taking a two-semester course?
- Do you have a bartering chip?

- Is there a question of embarrassment, shame, or powerlessness subtly built into your request?
- Is this actually about a power struggle, or does it really have some relation to what you want to change in him? Do you think that if you give in and do something for him, he'll slowly give you more and more things to do?
- Do you resent being made to feel like a nag, a mother, or a secretary? Should you be having a conversation about equality or about why it's actually taking him so long to take down the Christmas lights?

Prepare yourself for frustration. Even if you propose to make the change easier for him—"Let's put a calendar on the refrigerator, so you won't forget where you are supposed to be"—he still might not come around right away, if at all. There could be an adjustment period or a logjam. Only time will tell.

As the days pass, you and your man could continue to struggle for control. You have made a request that he is honoring, partially honoring, or completely ignoring, and this is likely to create some doubts in both your minds about who calls the shots here, anyway. He might act out. You might act out. Threats could come into play. Keep in mind what you have come to realize about his need for sticking to his guns; try to avoid being petty or passive-aggressive. Good luck with that.

Then there's the sex. Ah, to have sex or not to have sex when fighting. This is a decision that every couple ideally reaches mutually. On the one hand, many relationship experts suggest that it is unproductive to withhold sex from your romantic partner. On the other hand, you might not be interested in sex when you are feeling angry, and even if you are, it could be hard for you to reach orgasm. Although you should avoid using sex as a bargaining chip, you should also avoid sexual frustration. This is your call, but think about the steps you know are necessary to keep everything in perspective.

Slip-Slidin' Away

He's highly motivated to change a behavior that is deeply ingrained in his personality. Face the fact that this adjustment will take time and that he might slip back to his comfort level if his impetus wanes. It's not that he loses interest, it's just that the more comfortable (or less uncomfortable) he is, the less likely he will be to stick to the hard work of changing his behavior.

You may notice a little more reversion each day. Maybe the problem was his raising his voice—he's always been a loudmouth and was raised by loudmouth parents. Yesterday it was a decibel louder, today a bit more. When you point it out, he has a one-time excuse ("I didn't think they could hear me over the music!"), but you can already see his promise to change fading.

Maybe the issue is his packrat behavior, and he promises to work on it. It's smooth sailing for the first few weeks, but then you find a box in the trunk of his car, a desk he is "holding" for a friend in the garage, and the things that were going to the Salvation Army still gathering dust in his closet.

Maybe he's sneaky and passive-aggressive, so he lets you put a timer on the TV to help him monitor his couch-potato time. Then one day you catch him resetting the clock as you're coming out of the bathroom. He laughs it off, but you suspect that it happens all the time.

Perhaps he has promised to stop smoking, but when you lean down to kiss him, you swear you can detect the faint whiff of cigarettes. When you confront him, he tells you that you're just being paranoid. Not only do you now know that he's smoking again, his hesitation to admit it also makes you feel like a crazy person.

Ask him about the pace, or the slowing down, of change. It might be pure laziness, but it could have a history attached to it. Knowing the history can help him to differentiate between the past and the present, and it will enable you to be a bit kinder when he forgets. You think that it's perfectly reasonable to ask him to keep the bedroom clean, but every time you mention it, he explodes. It turns out that his dad was compulsively neat and constantly blew up about his untidiness. As a result, he swore he'd never let anyone tell him how to clean his own room.

You want him to dress nicer, but maybe his mom shamed him about spending money on himself. When you ask him to dole out some cash for a decent pair of shoes or a few dress shirts, you are fighting against years of ingrained guilt.

Perhaps you've accepted that he is always going to throw his clothes on the floor, so you've lowered the bar a bit. Now you just want the least amount of change that will make you happy: no wet towels mixed in, or the somewhat clean clothes thrown in a different pile from the dirty clothes.

You want to scream, "Look how flexible I am! Do you see how forgiving I am? I'm actually compromising with you!" Unfortunately, he is not going to recognize it. When the desired change behavior doesn't happen and he continues with the old bad behavior, you will become more exasperated than ever because you've reduced your demands and he still won't cooperate!

Motivating Him

If he wants you more than (or at least as much as) you want him, there are occasions in the future when he will be more motivated to change. (Even then, you risk the chance of his change being temporary.) Why don't you usually take advantage of this?

Your man's developmental stage will play a big role in motivation. It's a fact: Men will marry the woman standing next to them at the time of their lives that they decide they want to be married. You might be his soul mate, but if you're with him the year before this happens, you get zilch. A year later, when he's ready, he'll marry the woman standing in line behind him at the coffee shop, but when you were with him, he was still commitment-phobic.

What's responsible for this change? Here are some theories on how you might be able to make the change happen for you:

- *Successive approximations.* You praise him as he gets closer to the desired change. The drawback is that he recognizes this as an old parenting tactic.
- *Modeling.* You do what you'd like him to do. This works well with other women and in some group settings. A man, however, will probably think it's just something you like to do. The idea of exact reciprocity makes sense to you: if you are doing it, then why shouldn't he do it, too?
- *Reinforcement.* The white rat gets a pellet for every push of the bar. Even pigeons can be taught to play Ping-Pong with reinforcement, but it might be harder to find the perfect reinforcement for your man and carry it around in your bag. However, you might find other creative rewards.
- *Barter and bargain.* Diplomacy and practicality are key here. You want him to clean out the garage, and he wants you to clean out your child's old room so that he can put his golf bag and other sports equipment there. Shake on it, set a time frame, and get it done!
- *Power psychology.* The psychology of power and business will tell you that effecting change in a work setting is best achieved by making sure that the boss thinks that he or she has come up with the idea.
- *Dog-training tactics.* You paper-trained your adorable puppy. He sits, shakes, and rolls over because you are consistently

clapping, cooing, and offering snacks that taste like bacon. You do the same with your beau.

- *Child-rearing tactics*. You combine the psychological expertise of Benjamin Spock, Lawrence Balter, and *Chicken Soup for the Teenage Soul* to deal with disapproval, boundaries, age-appropriate behavior, peers, and the like.
- *Humor*. This is not the most evolved of tactics, but sometimes humor can minimize the pressure and get your point across. The problem is that he just might take your joke as, well, a joke.
- *Threats*. If you are bigger physically or control the cash, or if he's watched enough true-crime stories on TV about women who maim or murder in rage, he might respond to sentences that start with "If you don't . . ." However, you might get the opposite response if you directly challenge him and part of his brain lights up: confrontation! You could be talking about closing the cereal box so the cereal doesn't become stale or turning the TV off when he leaves the house, but he isn't going to budge, because it would feel to him like being knocked out in a boxing ring.
- *A dose of his own medicine*. He must not understand how infuriating his behavior is because he hasn't felt the consequences of it. Therefore, wouldn't giving him a dose of his own medicine work perfectly? Sorry, but he will never connect the dots. Even if the two situations are exactly the same, he won't get into your shoes and feel your pain, no matter what. His only response will be anger—period. Won't he feel just a little sympathy for you? Never.
- *Sex as a weapon*. This is a lose-lose situation. You get no sex. He gets no sex. Unfortunately for women, anger is a big libido killer.

Becoming a Nag

Becoming a nag is a very simple process. The first time you repeat yourself, you have become a nag, and then there is no going back. You repeated a request. Nag! You soften it with "Baby, I just wanted to remind you." Nag! Maybe you didn't say anything; you just let out an audible sigh as you picked up the dirty wet towel that he left lying on top of the clean folded clothes. He is bad, and you are good. Nag!

How do you get your point across without the *nag* label? Try the following:

1. Recognize when you are using a nagging tone: a sound that resembles a whine or the "I am repeating this because you are an idiot" sort of voice.
2. Notice his reaction. A dramatic eye roll, "I *know*," and a tortured look are all hints that you have entered the nag zone.
3. Can his doing what you want, or not doing what you hate, either make or break your day? You find yourself trying desperately to tell him telepathically, hoping that he does it.

Does this sound familiar? He has turned you into a nag, and/or you have jumped into the role of "the reminder," "the motivator," "the gatekeeper," "the mean nanny or babysitter," or, worst of all, "the laid-back girlfriend who has morphed into his mom."

Dealing with His Excuses

Maybe you are that one in a million who gets immediate cooperation when you tell a man what you'd like him to change and you give him an easy solution. That's probably not the case, however, and that's why you are reading this book. Let's look at some of his possible excuses:

1. "I work really hard; I don't want to do that when I get home. Bottom line: I've given the best at the office."
2. "You are exaggerating; it's your problem, not mine."

3. "I'm so tired; why are you busting my chops?"
4. "I'll do this only if you swear that there isn't a laundry list of things after it."

Tips and Tricks (for Not Being a Nag)

Can you agree on a subtle sign to use to remind him to take his fingers out of his mouth when you are out with friends? Will he consider that helpful, or will he become angry? Can you put a laundry basket (top open!) in the corner where he usually throws his dirty socks? There are more tactics, to be sure, but take a look at the following list and see which ones you have used before:

Tactics You Have Tried	His Response
Employing humor	Digs in his heels, engages in a power struggle
Pointing out how it looks to others	Is completely oblivious
Acting disappointed and wounded	Insists that it's a habit he can't control
Listing factual information	Shows annoyance at your picking something that he thinks is trivial
Removing yourself from the situation (ignoring the behavior)	Points out your equally annoying habit
Trying to figure out when it happens and then "teaching" him about it	Lists facts about why his behavior is okay
Suggesting substitute behaviors	Continues hoping that you'll give up
Employing positive reinforcement	Lies about not doing it as often
Using bribery	Insists that it's getting better

Tactics You Have Tried	His Response
Trying to show him how his behavior is incongruent	Engages in complete denial (what drinking problem?)
Trying to ignore his behavior but becoming resentful.	Puzzled as to why you are so pissy lately.

If any of the tactics listed above haven't worked, you could ask, "Sweetie, if I want you do something, like something around the house, what is the best way to ask you about it without making you feel embarrassed or irritated? I just don't want to be a nag about it." Of course, you might get some rather unhelpful answers, such as the following:

- "If you don't want to nag, then you do it."
- "If you don't want to nag, then don't remind me about it."
- "Don't put a big monologue in front of it; just say, 'Take out the garbage.'"
- "Don't start by apologizing, or it sounds as if you are not certain, and then I am not sure if you really want it."

What to Do When It Won't Stop

You've come full circle, and once again you are in negotiating mode. Once again you explain why you want and need this change. Write it down—for you and for him. Maybe he is saying, "Yes, I can do this now," or maybe you have decided to take a break while he works on it. Write it down. He will forget (or rather, it will become fuzzy), and you will forget (or rather, weaken in your resolve). Whether he keeps the list, you keep the list, or it goes on the fridge, it's important that you do it, no matter how corny it seems.

Here is an example of a list:

1. You will willingly go to two family events of mine a year.
2. You will stop biting your nails.
3. When you are going to be late coming home from work, you will call me if it's going to be more than an hour.
4. You will set a date by when you will have reached a certain benchmark.

This last item is important. Until now, whatever you've wanted has been undefined, or you've stretched it out another month and then another month, until you've lowered your expectations so much that you become upset only when his ICK pushes you to the brink. Then you think, "How did I get here?" To avoid this conundrum, the best thing to do is set a date for when he should have completed or achieved a mutually agreed upon goal. It doesn't have to be soon. Set a date, then add a month if it makes you feel good—but set a date.

Even if you end up adding more time, it will remind you that there is a contract, even it if was only with yourself and it was broken. Eventually it will help you to make a definite, hard decision. Maybe the decision will be "I choose to live with this, because it is never going to change. I've tried making a contract, and it's still not happening. The only change is that *I* am deciding to change, rather than to keep pining away."

Usually your conclusion will be the opposite: "He's not changing, even though that's what I need; he keeps promising, but obviously, nothing is moving. I'm out of here." Regardless, setting a defined time frame is essential.

Maybe you are not trying to convince him to change a behavior; rather, this time you want him to have a particular emotional response. You want him to be sensitive when you are upset or to respond more enthusiastically when your dad asks him a question. Unfortunately, his doing what you'd like will not necessarily mean that he actually feels either of these emotions for real. That may be okay with you sometimes, but when is it not? When will you become frustrated if what you wanted doesn't generalize to other situations because he only learned the shortcut?

You don't want him to stop being the essence of who he is, but you do want him to take a long, hard look at your list of demands and realize that these things are in *his* best interest. Before you corner him and get down to the nitty-gritty, you might want to assess his potential to really change. Can he do so? Does he have the motivation, the skills, and the personality?

To get started, ask yourself the following:

- What primary or secondary gain does he get from keeping the trait?
- What gain does he get from changing the trait?
- Is the trait something that can be put on a spectrum?

Then realize that there are two scenarios here:

- He agrees with you every time you mention it, then he continues to do it anyway. Your usual next step is to beg and to apologize for being irrational. You become angry.
- He changes for a minute, then goes back to the baseline. You show him that he has gone back to his old ways, and he sulks.

In an ongoing study that we are doing on relationships, women said that one thing that bothered them when they met the men in their lives never went away. It might have taken a different form, but it was often one of the main reasons they eventually broke up.

Outcomes

Review your list of desired or necessary changes and take a look at the scoreboard:

1. Total success. For example, he now uses floss to pick his teeth, and he does it in the bathroom! He calls when he is running late and seems apologetic. He realizes that his not telling the truth makes you feel terrible, so now he is exact and realistic in all of his answers.
2. Moderate success. This means more than 50 percent.
3. Mild success.
4. Failure.

Let's say you have mild success or failure. Now you have the knowledge that this situation is not going to change anytime soon, if ever. There is no more wishing, no more carrot dangling in front of your face. This is not great information, but it's very, very important information.

Here's another scenario: The guy you are dating is separated and has been saying that he's getting a divorce, but he's not doing it. He might do it down the line, but not on your timetable. That's bad news but a good realization. It gives you the same feeling you have when you finally get the news that your plane is not leaving the airport due to inclement weather. At least you aren't watching, waiting, and wondering anymore. Now you can make plans to stay another night, take a train, or get a hotel room and hit the bar.

It's the same with your guy. If he's a mild success or a failure, read the writing on the wall. Even if you decide to continue to wait, at least you have more straightforward information. So you *choose* to stay? That's fine, we aren't judging. As long as you do it fully informed and you aren't a victim of your own fantasies, your brain's tricks and illusions, and his cowardly way of continuing to give you hope, then it's a valid choice. He's not changing. If there is any possibility that he will, it's a very, very, very slim one. You may decide to put him on the back burner, give him another six months, or readjust your expectations, but at least you are not waiting around like a chump for the bus that isn't coming.

> **An Urban Myth or the Only Reality**
>
> The only time you can change men is when they are in diapers.

Can I Have It All? Do I Have to Lower the Bar?

If you had to choose, would you want a man who is three inches shorter than you but would never lie the way your man does? How about one who is really interested in your career but is terrible about doing chores around the house? How about one who is a clean fanatic around the house, even doing your chores, but is a bore in bed?

The next step is to look within yourself and assess your motivations and reactions:

- What is in it for me?
- What do I lose?
- What do I gain?
- What do I avoid?
- How much do I have to think about it?

As you narrow down the list about what makes you crazy, and you wonder whether you were right to see potential in your man, you should be discovering that you are also looking at what makes you tick in terms of helping, taming, developing, or teaching—whatever you want to call it—your significant other. Insight about yourself and foresight about his ability and motivation are what this is all about. Once you understand the role that your fantasy of Prince Charming plays, and you confront the consequences of thinking of yourself as a visionary, a sleuth, or a martyr who stands by her man no matter what, you will be sophisticated enough to see that you are part of a dysfunctional dynamic.

Will Missing the Boat with One Woman Change Him?

Women habitually think about all sorts of things that are upcoming. Men, on the other hand, think about something imminent only if it's a threat. For instance, women will go to a winter coat sale in August, but a man would be baffled at the mere suggestion. It's all about timing.

What if it turns out that the timing isn't right in your relationship, and you decide to walk away? "One man's loss is another man's gain," you think. "He'll die alone with his video games that drove me crazy. No one else would ever put up with him the way I have." Somewhere in the back of your mind, however, you wonder if you should have waited a little bit longer.

Mirror, Mirror on the Wall

As much as you might hate it, you have to ask yourself if you are winning the battle. Are you going to give ten more hours, ten more days, or ten more months to a man who might eventually become more sensitive, discover that he really does want children now, or scoff when he sees pictures of himself smoking cigars? If he really does have amazing traits that you love, why is a particular one so important to you?

Your girlfriends may agree with you. A cigar smoker? Gross—no way! He doesn't talk about his feelings? Oh, girl! He doesn't want children, or he wants more children? They may, however, wonder why you go ballistic when your generous adoring man needs a boys' poker night out, has to bring work home on the weekend, traipses into the kitchen in his work boots, or is still putting his toothbrush on the side of the sink instead of in the toothbrush rack. Why do you home in on things that might not bother someone else? What basis do you have for deciding that his "fault" is disgusting, gauche, or a sign that he is a boor?

"I realized that his not changing when I had asked him to had less to do about my request and more to do with my ego. I thought that he didn't respect me enough to change. He didn't think that way at all. When I defined *respect* and *respectful mate*, he was all that most of the time."

Moving On

Next time, you say, you'll do things differently. If you really mean it, you should make two pledges:

1. Change your priorities. For example, pick a guy who is sweet but who has some edgy hobbies rather than a tough guy who is sort of sweet in an erratic, unpredictable way. Rather than pick a wild and crazy guy who drives you nuts with his spontaneity, pick a grounded guy who has moments of being playful.
2. Don't ignore the red flags. State your requirements before ordering dessert on your first date. Even if you sound insane, you will know what you need before you waste any more of your life.

Deal Breakers

What happens if your differences are philosophical or ideological ones? The first rule is to give your man a keyword, such as

> "Somehow I ended up being the mom with the keys to the candy cupboard, so our relationship was all about whether he was good and I gave him candy or he wasn't and so I didn't. It had this added factor that I didn't want, and it made me into the bad guy."

code red, which means that this is a distinct and important situation. For example, you believe in the death penalty in certain circumstances, and he absolutely does not. You believe that abortion should be legal, and he is against it. He believes in heaven and hell, and you believe in reincarnation. If you are a defense lawyer, a gynecologist, or studying theology, these could be deal breakers; otherwise, you must make a pact to agree or disagree. In many ways, deal breakers are easier to deal with than other kinds of flaws, because they are so final.

Choose Your Battles

Everyone always says, "Choose your battles." "I won the battle but I lost the war" is another relevant fighting idiom. Your response that "this doesn't have to be a battle" just turns it into one. A simple task like changing the lightbulb in the hallway becomes a major melodrama.

Hear the Message

Perhaps he is saying, "This is stupid, I don't want to do this. I'm not doing it." Guess what? It means that he is not going to do it—period.

Be sure to listen. He will tell you how possible change is. Then add up the experience you've had using different molding techniques. What's your conclusion?

Check Yourself

The myth goes through your head again and again: if he loves me, he will change. Right? Wrong. To our female brains, the myth makes sense. If I love you, I will cook you things you like; I will

His History of Pleasing

Has he always been the bad guy whom everyone wanted to change? Has he always been the good guy who gave up his seat to someone else? Does he have to have a debate and understand *why* before he agrees to do it?

wear the underwear you like, even if it's uncomfortable; I'll laugh with your incredibly dull boss at the company party for hours.

Shouldn't this work both ways? The way you see it, you have points accumulated—lots of them, and you'd like to cash them in. "I'd like you to try wearing this snore tape on your nose one night, or take the air conditioners out now that it's November, or get that weird mole looked at, please," you say to him. He puts it off, makes excuses, pretends he didn't hear you. He must not love you, you conclude. How did you get into this one-sided relationship with a man who can't play fairly?

One thing that won't work is the notion that you'll lead by example. That will definitely mess you up. He will see it as "you choose to do this, and I choose to do that."

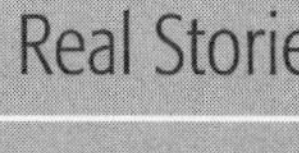

Real Stories

"Frankie would do the laundry halfway. He'd put it in the washer and then forget about it. I'd either have to rewash it or he'd finally notice and put the smelly wash in the dryer. It was more work for me to remind him than to just do it myself. It ended up that I did most of the housework myself."

"Mike slouched. I loved how tall he was, and although he had been too tall as a kid, his height was great as an adult. His slouching was terrible for his back pain, plus it looked bad. I would straighten him out, but I had to do it constantly."

"I do think that Casey's not doing what I ask is emotional. He knows it bothers me but chooses not to do it anyway. We go back and forth with the same old story. I tell him not to bite his nails and explain that they look awful, it's dirty, and it really, really bothers me. I give him examples of things that I have changed that he didn't like. His response is to argue with me about why it bothers me. Who cares *why* it bothers me? It infuriates me that despite everything, he thinks that I will drop it if he sees that I accept that he's not going to change."

Make-up sex, as we've said before, is a bad idea. Given that change and excitement is a libido booster, you may find yourself picking fights just to have more exciting sex, but it's a negative thing, in the long run, if you have to pick a fight in order to have a good orgasm.

If a man is already in trouble with you for being an hour late, sometimes the idea of just not coming home till dawn seems to be a better remedy. Women believe that if he would only understand, he would change. If he would only understand what it feels like to have to wait, he wouldn't do it to you again. That is why, when you see a couple arguing on television, she always seems to be tortured by his failure to understand how she feels.

Remember That You Love Him

Are you quiet about the things you love about him, and do you mention only the things you want him to change? Do you praise as well as criticize? Does he take the praise as criticism?

Is it really true that you should give both good and back feedback? Has your entire dynamic gone from chatting and laughing together to your either praising him or reprimanding him in an attempt to corral him as if he's a border collie racing from left to right?

Remind him of what you like about him. You love him. There's no question about that, but it's easy for him to lose sight of that when you are so focused on the negative. It's important not to turn into someone who is so nitpicky that he thinks he will never be able to please you.

"Once forced to look at why I had become such a nag, I realized that this is the way that people in my family spoke to one another. We were another version of *Everybody Loves Raymond*. My therapist told me to notice how often I was complaining about my boyfriend to someone else and how often I was nagging him to do something. I was mortified to see that our entire relationship was starting to revolve around this dynamic."

8 Know When to Walk Away, Know When to Run

Have you ever have a hard time deciding whether you should stay at a party another hour or simply get up and leave because you know you need to get some sleep (and probably nothing exciting is going to happen)? In every situation, you weigh the pros and cons—you can see the benefits of staying, and you can see the benefits of leaving. So you go back and forth; you are sitting on the proverbial fence. You hope that something will pull you in one direction or the other, because the indecision is torturous. If you leave, you might miss something good. If you go, you won't beat yourself up for staying too long and feeling foolish for having wasted time.

It's the same with relationships. You finally see the relationship scale teeter back and forth and settle right in the middle: fifty-fifty. It's no longer tipped in his favor. Before, it would go back and forth: up a bit, then down a bit. At least when he was at 51 percent, he was mathematically over the line. Then the day arrives when he's at 49 percent, 47 percent, or 42 percent, and you would be blind not to see that you spend more time being frustrated by him and fighting with him than liking him and having a good time. Numbers don't lie.

You have two diametrically opposed feelings that are constantly beating each other up, like angry cartoon characters trying to take center stage. This is what goes through your head:

1. "Leave, you sniveling fool. You are turning into the kind of woman you hate. You know, the kind who goes back and forth, who bores her girlfriend with every detail of what her man did and didn't do. There are millions of men out there; you are wasting time. He is not changing. It couldn't be clearer—and if he *can* change, it's not going to be anytime soon, and it has nothing to do with your asking. It is driving you crazy. Pack. Leave. Don't look back."
2. "Sure there are tons of guys out there, but this guy is your soul mate. How can you throw out real love? How can you lose hope in him and your relationship? If you give up, you'll regret it for the rest of your life. Then someone else will get this great guy. You'll die alone and never forgive yourself. Besides, it's really not that bad. You are oversensitive. Hang in there; it will get better."

You are not alone. You know these scenarios all too well, because more than once you have lent a friend a shoulder to cry on. "He's driving me crazy, I have to get out," she'd tell you. "He's a jerk," you'd agree. Maybe you'd even add a pejorative adjective or two in order to rile her up a bit more and motivate her to move on. Off she'd go to pick up her stuff at his house, only to cancel plans with you later because she had decided to stay over at his house. You can't keep from sighing out loud when she says something like the following:

"Don't worry, this time he knows I am serious."

"I am giving him one more week, seven days, and that is it."

"I read him the riot act, and he gets it now."

"We talked. I just need to ease up and have some faith. Everybody has stuff to work on. I'm not perfect, either, you know."

"We just had the best sex. I'm staying a little while longer—just a little."

Soon the postfight honeymoon goes flat; tension rises, mounts, and explodes; and the old dynamic starts all over again. Is he really showing some effort? What feedback are you getting from people around you? Each time you fight, do you also learn how to problem-solve, or is it just another variation of the argument before?

"There were moments I would have bet anything that it was over. In my head I was 100 percent out. Then, gradually, I'd get over it, my anger would wither, and I'd sort of 'forget' why I was leaving so suddenly, or it would seem like not such a big deal. I'd go from fuming and wanting to kill him to feeling helpless and resigned and confused. I thought I was losing my mind; I just couldn't stay in one frame of mind."

His Reaction

You've probably told him, in one way or another, that you are really, really fed up. Maybe you've even broken up once already. Maybe you've

> "I started having jealousy dreams, then I realized that part of me wanted to catch him doing something really wrong, because then I'd have the excuse to go. I'd be absolutely right. In the dream I'd be livid but somewhat relieved as well."

walked out so many times that you don't even bother to unpack your bag; you just leave it by the door, ready for after the next fight. He either breaks down every time you leave and insists that he can't live without you or, by this point, simply shrugs and motions for you to move away from in front of the TV screen. If you are having explosive fights, each one feels more exhausting. Maybe you are having the same conversation over and over, or maybe you just have the conversation with yourself in your head and grit your teeth.

Part of you wants to grab him by the shoulders, shake him, and make him tell you, plain and simple, if he is going to do what you want. "Stop lying! Stop cheating! Stop drinking! Stop putting me down! Stop procrastinating! Stop right there! I gotta know right now! Before we go any further, what's it gonna be, boy—yes or no?"

His reaction might be one or more of the following:

- He bargains, then doesn't keep up his end of the deal.
- He tells you that this is who he is, that *you* have to change.
- He tells you that you are imagining these problems, so get some help.
- He says to give him some time, that he's working on it.
- He doesn't say much, which leads you to (mistakenly) believe that he is thinking about it.
- He tells you that the two of you have love and that everything else is petty.

- He seems exasperated; he walks into the bathroom, and you hear him get into the shower (he's definitely thinking about it now, right?).
- He dramatically pulls himself off the couch and yells, "This is what you want, right? Fine! I'll get a job, I'll work at Starbucks if it will make you happy!" He grabs his jacket and stomps out of the house, slamming the door behind him. Four hours later he returns, doesn't tell you where he was until you ask, and then responds that he filled out six job applications. They'll call him. He gets a beer from the refrigerator and sits down on the couch again.

"I'd go back and forth, saying to myself, 'What you are asking for is not a big deal; any guy would be more than happy to do this to be with you,' then 'Why am I so stuck on these stupid things for him to change? He's a good guy, and I'm not going to do better, so why can't I just accept him the way he is?' It was like having an insane conversation with three people, all of whom were me."

Desperate for Perspective: How to Get Off the Fence

At times you wish that some genie or fairy godmother would come around and say, "Stick it out. He's worth it—you'll see." At other times you wish she'd show up and say, "What's wrong with you? Get out of here—you are wasting your time!" At still other times you are desperate to know what you two look like from the outside. Are you like the couples you see on reality TV who think they are being so passionate and dramatic but just look ridiculous? Could someone objectively look at your boyfriend and see why it would be hard to give him up? Could someone look at you two and think that you really do have to figure it out, because you're such a great couple? Or are you the kind of couple that people look at and roll their eyes?

Once you decide to look at your situation objectively, there are a few steps you can take:

1. Start a journal that chronicles everything. *Be sure to put it somewhere safe.* In it, write the following:
   - What you have said to him, what you think he heard, and his response
   - How this was similar to or different from last time. Put down dates and times.
   - What you wish would happen
   - What your friends and family say about him
   - What your friends and family say about your relationship

   The point of writing all this down is to keep things clear in your head. You didn't hallucinate his response, you did give it almost a month, and you have dates to prove it to yourself. Writing all this down will help you to keep your sanity.

2. Give him a clear list in writing. We have said this before, but it bears repeating. You may write the list in shorthand in front of him, but do put it down in black and white. When you have finished talking to him, summarize: "There are [add number] things I am asking you to do." Make sure that you are doing this when you feel good communicating. You need to hear him say one of the following: "Yeah, of course I can do that; don't worry about that, please"; "That one? That is no big deal. Go ahead and write it if you want. But consider it done"; "That is the stupidest request I have ever heard, but fine, if that is what you want, I'll do it, just to prove to you that I can"; or "I don't see how I can get that done, but I'll try; I'll take some steps and see about that."

- Set dates by which your requests should be fulfilled. None of the things on the list can be open-ended. If he wants to start on Monday rather than today, that's fine, just put down the date.
- As much as you want to remind him about the impending date, you can't remind him. He told you he would do this, let him do it or not do it.

3. Maybe you have broken up and are talking about what it would take to get back together. Again, write a list. It shouldn't be a threat or a punishment, just an honest list of things he has to do in order for the relationship to move forward. You'll often find that the list has several requests that are all for his own good. For example:
   - "Stop biting your fingernails; sure, I hate it, but it looks ugly to professional people around you at work."
   - "No drinking and driving; you'll hurt yourself or someone else and/or end up in jail."
   - "Pay off your credit cards once and for all; you are losing money paying fines and interest."
   - "Stop using the word *dude* all the time; you are an adult, and you sound like a stoned surfer."

Deciding to walk away from a man you love can be extremely difficult. Even battered women sometimes go back to their abusers several times before making a clean break. It's a process. Part of you has to be totally convinced that he's not going to change and that you really can't just let his behavior go, no matter how much you try. Part of you also has to go through the experiment of trying to not let the ICK bother you, only to realize that it does, when you start having migraines.

Real Stories

"I've found myself asking my friends for advice. 'Be brutal,' I'd say. Then when a friend starts to tell me my boyfriend's shortcomings and what she thinks of us, I feel myself wanting to argue with her and show her that she's wrong. Yet I was the one asking for the advice!"

"I'd think about the future without him, and, I'm embarrassed to say, I'd feel panicky. I knew that I wouldn't die without him, and I knew that I would look back and see these moments later in life as part of my growing up in some way, but it was the near future, this week and the next two, that made me want to run away. I really thought that I had to leave the country if I was going to get away from him. It wasn't that *he* was making me go back. It was something inside me that I was fighting."

"I decided that I was not going to let his being a slob bother me. So what if he always gets food on his sleeve while he's eating dinner? He is sweet and funny and does everything else right. His whisker stubbles are constantly in the sink, but there are worse things than that. It's not going to change. I can be thankful that he wears long sleeves only in the winter and that our next place will have two bathrooms."

"I made the decision that I was not going to let his flirting get to me. I saw him watch a woman in a pair of shorts walk by, and I just gritted my teeth. He winked and smiled at the bank teller, and I could feel my chest tighten. He's not changing; I have to change. The problem is that although I don't show that I am angry, it boils up inside me. I can't stop my reaction. I'm going to end up with an ulcer if I continue like this."

Decide!

By the time you reach this chapter, you should have some perspective on why you entered this relationship and what kinds of things are keeping you here. He has potential—from a minuscule, pea-size amount to absolutely seething with it and soon to become the next superman incarnate. He does have an ICK, however, or maybe several ICKs. You've sized him up on the scales, done the math, and answered all of the questions we've thrown at you. The choices of what you can do now aren't endless; the possibilities aren't infinite. Actually, you have alternatives from which to choose right now:

1. Brush it off. You will not let his quirk bother you, or at least you will console yourself with his good traits and know that it is something that you have *decided* to tolerate. Some miracle may happen to extinguish the ICK, but you are not betting on it, so when he does whatever it is, you simply sigh and remember something you like about him.
2. Remind him—forever. You aren't letting it go, you are going to keep trying new tactics, whatever it takes. He will never handle it consistently, but you can't just let it go. You *choose* not to let it go. It annoys you, and you are going to stay and enjoy him, but you're also going to continue your irritating quest to rid him of his ICK. Be prepared to be accused of nagging.
3. Set a date—with the moving people. It doesn't have to be next week, but do set a date so that you can evaluate any progress and renegotiate. During a honeymoon time, you wrote your list and agreed on a date by which he would have done (or stopped doing) the activities in question. Now it's that date, so you sit down, bring out the list, and start listening to his excuses. Once you realize that very little has changed, that slap in the face of reality will take the place of your wishy-washy feelings or lack of clarity. You might renegotiate and set a date three or four times, but each time you'll feel clearer about what has the potential to change and what doesn't.

The point of this is not to let yourself be thrown around like Dorothy in the tornado. Maybe you decide not to let his behavior bother you, but then you find that it does, so you change your mind and decide that you are going to do something else besides waiting and trying to keep your balance on the fence. Write down your reactions—with details. Reread what you wrote. Realize that little, if anything, has changed. Make a note of what worked for a while.

You are not being held in the relationship against your will, so make a decision, even if it is just to reevaluate in three months. You can keep dating him, knowing all the things you know now, but set a date for when the situation has to be resolved. Otherwise, work on having it really (not just on the surface) not bother you because you've found other things you really love about him, and they tip the scale way, way over in his direction.

The point is not to feel pushed one way or another and confused about what you feel or who you are anymore. You might have to read a particular chapter over again and be more honest with yourself this time. Rather than feeling like a victim, you should understand the dynamics better, see how your choices are affecting you, and really be able to assess his good and bad traits diplomatically.

Make sure that you have all the facts straight, and then answer the following questions:

1. Do you find that you are anxious when you are in a situation where he might do the ICK? (You are watching to see if he looks at other women, you're on high alert when he is supposed to be sober and he's out with his friends, you check his pockets for gambling stubs while holding your breath, you pray that he won't chew with his mouth open while you're at dinner with your friends.)

2. Does training, changing, or molding him feel like a part-time job? When you are trying to figure out what he is

thinking, are you going through scenarios in your head of how you could explain it better?

3. Do you find that you can't have one conversation with a friend that doesn't include some recent occurrence or irritating moment with him?
4. Does the real you feel lost in this process? Do you think back to the days when you were single and carefree?
5. Do you feel almost tortured by this makeover project or your indecision about it? Are you unhappy with what a nag, worrywart, or whiny woman you have become?
6. Do you find yourself fantasizing that the decision has been made for you? Do you spend way too much time on the pity pot?

Walk Away

Sometimes walking away—even for just six months or a year—can give you a tremendous amount of information on the man you've been dating and what you want in a boyfriend, a husband, or a life partner. If you then decide that it is the right move to walk away, you may run into your ex five years later and find yourself having one of the following reactions:

- "I still think he's a good guy in his heart—not for me, but a really great guy for someone else."
- "He looks good, but I know he's slippery, and I really adore the guy I have now. I'm glad I made this choice."
- "Incredible! So much time has passed, and he is still a jerk. I am so glad that I didn't keep beating myself up by being in that relationship."
- "Coffee tomorrow? Sure, I'd love to."

Soul Mate

A soul mate is not necessarily the person with whom you were "meant" to be. A soul mate can be anyone, regardless of age and gender, with whom you "click" and who understands you effortlessly. The perfect husband for you does not have to be a soul mate, and a soul mate may not be the best husband for you. The idea that fate brings you together, that you are perfectly in sync with a soul mate, and that there is only one person for you in the entire world is a myth and a fantasy. Soul mates still have to work to get along in daily life.

Q and A

Q I still can't decide for sure if I want to leave, but at least I have a clearer understanding of the traits that are important to me. Without selling myself short and without letting it eat me up inside, I'm going to see what the next few weeks bring. Is it okay that I am not being definitive yet?

A Yes, being in a relationship is a process, and getting out is a process. Even breaking up, living apart for a year or more, and finding each other again might be part of the process. It will seldom happen that you can make a really definitive choice about someone and never want to change it again. Even with people who have angered you, there should come a time to forgive them and move on. Maybe you will be civil or even friendly again. The idea of absolute closure is not usually realistic. In your case, continuing to define and understand what you want is part of your process. Don't beat yourself up for it.

Q Sometimes I wonder if I am lying to myself. When I say or write something, I have to check myself and make sure that I am telling the truth. Is that odd?

A That isn't odd. Your ability to see the problem from different perspectives at different times can muddle how you feel about it. Just keep in mind that your perception of it can change. Make a note to yourself when it does change and see if there are any patterns. Understanding yourself better is the goal here.

Q Is it okay to say that we are just taking a break from each other when I am actually hoping that it will be a final breakup?

A Sometimes, saying *breakup* feels like a death. *Taking a break* can be more bearable for both of you. Unfortunately, it can also keep feelings and fantasies alive, and one of you may end up getting hurt by thinking the break was temporary. It could also get in the way of your really spending time apart.

Q How can I make myself become fed up? I am almost there, but I never get quite totally sick of it—at least, not enough to leave.

A Keeping a journal can help tremendously. When you reread it and recall how hurt you were at different times, it will become clearer to you how much and how needlessly you are suffering. Once you have written pages and pages over time, you'll become more motivated to put your foot down, to leave the relationship, or to change your own perspective.

Feeling Like a Fool

You stick it out, stick it out, and stick it out. After weeks, months, and maybe even years, you finally crash and burn and break up. Then you look back and see the time you wasted and become really angry with yourself. You alternate feeling incensed at him for leading you on and at yourself for being a sucker. How could you have wasted so much time? You beat your head against the wall, watching the movie play out in your head. You are agonizing, crying, spending month after month bawling your eyes out.

Hold it right there. Don't go into postrelationship victim mode. This could eat you up inside just as much as being in that lousy situation would. Realize that there is no such thing as wasted time or missed opportunities; it just wasn't the right time. This is no joke. You stayed as long as you needed to, as long as your brain and your soul needed to learn something.

Are you still ambivalent about him? You aren't finished, then. Figure out exactly why you are staying, what attracts you, where you want things to be, and when you want change to happen. Draw a line in the sand for what you will tolerate and what you want, then stick to it. Then the next time he disappears for the whole night, you catch him in a lie, or he picks a fight with your sister, you can call him on it loud and clear, and maybe it will be the thing that pushes you over the edge. If it's a more minor issue, maybe you'll just sigh, pick up the toothpaste cap off the floor, and plan to buy a pump tube after that.

Knowing When It's Time to Go

"The best things are worth working for" isn't really true here. Has he actually taken steps to change, or have you lowered your expectations so much that he gives you that illusion? Have you become so obsessed with "winning" or finishing your "project" that you have completely lost track of how you actually feel about him right now? Has he made actual strides to change, and are they permanent, or will he slip back into his old patterns? Know when to stop pushing, be satisfied with what you learned, and walk into the sunset with no regrets.

He Throws You a Bone: Too Little, Too Late

What happens if he won't change, but he won't let you go? It's hard to resist when someone acts as if they'll die without you. He begs you not to leave, but he still refuses to hear *your* pleas. The hard truth is that if it's bad enough for you to consider leaving, then the situation has to change. Otherwise, the resentment will build and build, and your relationship will be rife with conflict. Explain this very simple fact to him. If that doesn't motivate him, then you have your answer.

Even when you know that it's time to move on, it doesn't mean that suddenly life will become easy. Attachments, even to a man who is not good for you, can run deep. If there weren't an overwhelming sense of connection and a feeling of entanglement, you wouldn't have stuck around as long as you did. Time is a good teacher. Knowing when to walk away is one of the hardest things you'll ever have to figure out.

If the Quirk Irks, Face It

Lisa knew from the beginning that James wasn't her ideal man, but he was kind to her and loved her more than any man had loved her before. During the year that they dated, the little quirks that she thought she could overlook started to irk her more and more. Whereas she jumped out of bed at 7 a.m. to go for a run, he slept till noon and puttered around the house for hours. She thought he was just going through a phase, so she began to harness her energy into helping him break out of his stale routine. After a few months of failed attempts, Lisa thought that maybe James's devotion to her made their lifestyle difference barely noticeable. By the end of the year, however, she saw that even his undying love couldn't convince her to stay.

(continued)

If your man has scored abysmally low on all of our scales—that is, you've found yourself answering no or "not really" or "maybe when hell freezes over" to our questions on his moldability—then no radical moves are going to change him. Maybe you are dead set on it: you are going to change this man or die trying. You will handcuff him to you, you will get pregnant, you will tattoo his name on your neck. That is a bad, bad idea. You'll end up with a resentful partner who is there—perhaps only temporarily—because you have cornered him.

Q and A

Q I love my guy unconditionally. Once he realizes this—that I am the only one who would give him a kidney if he needed it—he will change, right?

A Unless he needs a kidney and you give it to him, the fact that you would do so is of little importance to him. Because you say you love him unconditionally and would give him a body part if he needed it, is he going to think that he should try to get along with your friends, spend less time watching TV, or lose fifteen pounds? Not likely.

Q My boyfriend came from a terrible family, and his mother didn't love him. Once he realizes that my love can heal him, everything will be okay, right?

A Love can heal only when it's coupled with self-love. You can support him and show him that you care, but you will not be able to motivate or encourage him to have better self-esteem unless he is doing therapy work on his own.

Q My guy is clingy and needy. If I give him more attention, he is like a bottomless pit; if I give him less and encourage him to be independent, he sulks, says I don't love him, or gets angry. Thoughts?

A This is a difference in your relating styles that is going to be very hard to negotiate. The first step is to try to pinpoint what he wants and when, and when he feels more independent. You may need to find out whether he has heard this from past girlfriends and whether it's something he'll consider working on on his own. The neediness may come from some experience very early in his childhood, and you are right in thinking that this could end up being a bottomless pit that you will never be able to fill on your own, no matter how much you try.

Q Can life events, such as a friend getting lung cancer or a hurricane blowing down his house, make a man change?

A Life events can cause your man to come around temporarily, but there are no guarantees that they will have a lasting effect. In the case of a boyfriend who smokes, having a friend develop lung cancer may just be the "nail in the coffin," so to speak. Many times, the threat of death can freak someone out enough that he'll change his bad habits. Otherwise, if the threat is on a more superficial level—he nearly loses his job due to his repeated lateness, or he is almost sideswiped by a car while he's riding his bike because he wasn't paying attention—permanent change isn't as likely. The reason for this is that as time passes, memories begin to fade. For a week or two, he may show up to work on time or stay alert on the road, but after the threat wears off, he'll start to relax and will once again revert to his old ways.

Q I've started dating again and don't want to make the same mistakes. What do I have to remind myself of?

A Heed the danger signs. There are men who, no matter how much hard labor you invest in them, will always let you down.

The five types who are most likely to resist your good intentions are: (1) the guy who thinks you are being irrational or petty when you try to change him; (2) the guy who says he's trying, but he's dragging his feet; (3) the guy who changes temporarily, but soon enough he's back to his old ways; (4) the guy whose pride is in the way and who doesn't want to lose a fight; and (5) the guy who defines himself by the very trait you want him to change. You have two choices with these men: accept them as they are or get out of the "ring"—now!

Giving Up the Fantasy: The Thoughts That *You* Need to Change

As you are trying to move on, there are thoughts that creep into your head that pull you back. Stop thinking of yourself as defeated or spineless; start trying to see your situation as something that although it might feel pretty crummy right now, can get a whole lot better.

You think: At this point—feeling stuck between wanting to go and wanting to stay—if you go, you have to lose the fantasy of what your future was going to look like with him in it.

Change to: Change your self-image from spinster or single to "unattached." The possibilities for you are endless. He didn't want to take a dance class, and you want more than anything to have a boyfriend who will tango. Go for it now!

You think: It seems as though the relationship was in vain. You worked and waited, and it still failed. Part of you wants to keep trying rather than admit defeat.

Change to: There is no such thing as defeat in relationships. Every relationship is an attempt to learn more about yourself and how to get along with someone better.

You think: You love the stories about how you met; one wonderful weekend you had keeps you together. You tell that story over and over, only to conclude that the things you love about your relationship are really just a few details. It's a broken relationship with moments that seemed magical.

Change to: Stop sniveling. So you had some good times; that doesn't mean you should stay with a man who doesn't work for you, just because two years ago you had a great vacation together and have the pictures to prove it. If you aren't having enough good times now, then call a spade a spade. The lusty moments you had in phase one of love will definitely make it into your memories.

You think: "I am such a spineless twit."

Change to: Maybe at this point you have tallied up all the information and can say realistically, "I am not out of hope, I am not sick enough yet, or really, I think this relationship can be salvaged." This is not a sign of your being soft, stupid, or brainwashed.

Q and A

Q I hate who I have become in this relationship; I don't even recognize myself anymore. Sometimes I doubt that I'd like this man even if I convinced him to do what I have wanted, since it's taken so long. If I leave, however, I'll think that I am abandoning him. Is there someone better for him out there?

A Marlene Dietrich once said, "Most women set out to try to change a man, and when they have changed him, they do not like him." This is especially true if the trait you wanted to change was a symptom of his problem, or if the time and effort you've expended have become so huge and complex that you are exhausted. The idea that he will be lonely without you is absurd. He will be out having fun before you come to the end of this sentence. There is definitely a woman (at least one!) out there who either does the same annoying things he does or who is completely unfazed by his quirks.

Q I am making my guy change, come hell or high water. I've already made the decision for him. I know I can change him, because I am tougher than other women. Determination is everything, right?

A Stop. You are making a disturbingly common mistake. Whether you think you can change him because you're tougher, more special, or more deeply connected to him than any other woman has been, you're wrong. You could be all or some of those things, but none of them will make him change. Whether he changes is not a reflection on you. When someone changes, it is always on his terms. You may have been the one to initiate it, or you may nudge him along, but people have to change on their own. If you continue to measure yourself by whether he changes, it can have negative effects on your confidence and self-esteem.

What Would You Change—in Yourself?

How willing are you to look at change as just part of evolving as a person? Answer the following with a firm yes or no (no waffling):

1. Are there any traits or behaviors of your own that you would like to change?
2. Are you typically set in your ways?
3. When was the last time you gave something up—for a New Year's resolution, per someone's request, or just to see if you could?

Thanks for the Reminder!

Peter Kramer, author of *Should You Leave?*, talks about gifts that can be clear indicators from your partner that you should go. Really, these are virtual presents that give you clarity, almost unequivocally, that the relationship is over. Reminders—the memories that you associate with the break-up, with getting back together, with why you left and, in fact, why you should still be gone—are a gift, as well.

4. Do you view relationships as partnerships, or do you think that one or the other partner usually has the upper hand?
5. If someone told you that you had something stuck between your teeth, would you be thankful, or would you be embarrassed and wish that she hadn't said anything? If someone else had something stuck between her teeth, would you tell her?

The Other Side of the Fence: Going Back

It's Saturday night and you have plans with your friends, or maybe you are having a "you" night: taking a bath, listening to your favorite music, and relaxing. A certain man keeps sneaking into your thoughts. "I wonder what he's doing. I wonder if he is thinking of me." Then slowly, you let yourself think about going back. You ponder the following:

1. You know that he loves you, in his own way. He may just need time to realize how much he misses you and how little you are asking him to do. Maybe you just didn't explain what you wanted well enough.

2. It seems as though your brain and your heart aren't in agreement. They are like two little children with whom you are trying to bargain.
3. You've done an emotional "Photoshop": your brain automatically deletes him from your future, and it's as if you are looking at a wedding picture or a family vacation photo in which one person's head has been cut out.

9

Getting Over Him

Finally, you want out—not out of the argument or out of the house, but *out* out. Maybe he's still lying, still cheating (or almost cheating), still unresponsive to your requests, and still uninterested in what you call growing together. Maybe the trigger was yet another fight over the many things he refuses to change (or the simple one that he thinks is asinine). These disappointments have become the straw that broke the camel's back. You've been here a million times before, but this time is different. This is *the end*—no sequel, epilogue, or cryogenic freezing to enable a return. Unequivocally, the credits are rolling, the curtain is closing, and the show is over.

The reason it has taken you so long to find the neon-lit red exit sign after so many near misses is the unfortunate truth that you probably don't want to leave him. That's why you've given him 101 opportunities to change. He is so close to being perfect yet so damn far from addressing the one thing that is really important to you. You've made it so clear, spelling out exactly what reasonable things he would have to do to maintain the relationship. You've handed it to him on a platter, making it so that he'd have to put forth only the tiniest effort. You made compromises and sacrifices and came up with all kinds of justifications. "He's just distracted, he's so tired, he's really working hard, his plate is full right now," you've told yourself and others. "He'll get to it, I know he will, just give him a chance, he has to fully digest." Your friends and your family have either gone along with it, rolled their eyes behind your back, or insulted you in a way that made you feel a keener need to stand by his side.

Now you've come to this chapter, and it's a slap in the face, but you really aren't surprised. You've accepted the fact that he isn't changing at all, or if he is, it's halfheartedly, or if it's enough, it's only temporary. You've decided that you can't or don't want to live with things the way they are. You've tried to ignore it, to talk yourself out of how important it is to you, and to list the pros and cons on paper to show yourself how silly you are being. Your brain has tallied things up, and the scales are not tipped in his direction anymore. You are fed up with his leading you on, you are fed up with how naive you've been, and you have come to the conclusion that this is one big lesson you'll never have to learn again.

Your heart is in smithereens. You've been holding it together with thread and tape. He seemed so close. He seemed as if he had—ugh, say it—potential. Finally, you know that there's no point in giving him more time, explaining it better, picking the right time to bring it up, or making it more attractive. You pack your bags (or his), clean out the drawers and the shelf in the bathroom, throw away (or shred) the pictures on your desk, and get ready for the next few days or weeks of the hellish "getting over him" process.

This is the worst kind of breakup. You can't really hate his guts, because he's just doing everything as he has before. In a weird sort of way, you feel sorry for him: he is losing you because he's too stubborn or stupid to realize how much his behavior means to you.

What happens next? Are you the "hide under the covers" type? The "drink and eat ice cream like Bridget Jones" type? Or the "tie one on with your friends and wake up with the bouncer from the bar in your bed" type? Planning for dramatic self-pity can make it slightly easier; at least you'll tell your friends what to expect and stock up on your favorite fat-laden and sugary snacks. Let's look at a few scenarios:

1. You hold the letter L (for loser) to your forehead for the next week. You call yourself all kinds of self-deprecating names. Sometimes, in an extra spurt of drama, you curl up on the floor and say ridiculous things like "Who is going to love me as much as he did?" "I'll never be happy again," or "What did I do to deserve this?" Although you don't really believe it wholeheartedly, you are amused (slightly) by how dramatic you can be. You sleep. You drink hard liquor or take any over-the-counter drug that professes to make you sleep.

   When you wake up you feel horrible, which actually makes you feel better, because now at least your physical and your mental states agree with each other. Sometimes you answer the phone, but only when you know it's your kind, sensitive friends, not the "get your act together, you don't have cancer" ones. The next day you spend a good ten minutes poking at the puffy bags under your eyes, wondering if they will affect your peripheral vision. You are amazed at the quantity of tears your body can produce and swear you'll research it when you feel better. As soon as you hear the Muzak version of Cyndi Lauper's "Time after Time" in the elevator, you start crying again. The same goes for the songs of Phil Collins or Neil Young or anything with sentimental lyrics.

2. You turn into Satan—not the cute little red devil who sits across from the angel on your other shoulder; it's the bloodthirsty one with long red nails who wants to annihilate the world and leave it scarred and barren forever. You are furious and vindictive. You can't concentrate on work; instead you fantasize about pouring sand in your ex's gas tank; putting a hex on his house, and spreading nasty rumors about him.

   How dare he take you for such a fool? How dare he brush away your heartfelt love with such disregard? He should be groveling at your feet right now, sobbing for a second chance. Your anger keeps you up at night. You fight the temptation to throw things across the room. You sing Alanis Morissette's "You Oughta Know" four or five times a day. You console yourself with the knowledge that his karma will catch up with him, and then you imagine all the ways he would suffer as you stepped over him on your way to your next date.

3. You hum "Love Stinks" and keep your schedule as regular as possible. Gym, work, food—it's business as usual. You can't control him or your emotions, but there is still the 6:30 p.m.

spin class and the dry cleaning to pick up. You pull yourself up by your bootstraps, keep a stiff upper lip, and prepare to ride out the storm. You use this as an excellent excuse to purge your closets and repaint your apartment. You join a dating Web site and keep moving as fast as you can so that you don't have time for self-pity.

Your friends are suspicious, not satisfied with your pat answer that you are now really free to find yourself again. You repeat mantras like "Onward and upward," "It was just a matter of time," "In retrospect, I think he did me a favor," and similar unconvincing party lines that no one really believes. There's no point in dwelling on him. Sometimes you break down, but you try not to let anyone else see. You vacillate between missing him and reminding yourself that time will make it better.

Recovery Stages

Just as accepting death or kicking an addiction is a process with stages or steps, breaking up is a process, too. After talking to hundreds of patients and answering questions from magazine and newspaper readers, focus groups, and, of course, friends, we've come up with five breakup recovery steps.

As with every other process, most people start at the beginning, then spend a short or a long time in each stage, depending on their experience and support system. Finally, they make it to the end or get as close to it as they can. As with any series of steps, you can relapse, fall off the wagon, lose your "sober" days, or just slip a few steps back, because something triggered you and made you stagger or even sent you flying with what felt like a kick in the chest. You might sit there trying to catch your breath, feel embarrassed or pitiful, or just brush yourself off and start all over again, because you've been here before and you'll probably be here again. You know, however, that one day you'll be able to look back and feel some kind of peace, resolution, or perspective.

Some people say that it takes half the time you were together to really get someone out of your system. Others say four seasons. Some say that if a bigger, better deal sweeps you off your feet the weekend after, it's a "get out of jail and pass go" kind of bonus. The point is that there are individual differences.

You should personalize the following list and note how and when you have trouble and become stuck at different stages.

1. *Shock.* You might not be pallid, shivering, and walking around with a blanket over your shoulders, but after a big breakup you could still find yourself in shock. It's the feeling, maybe even a numb one, that you survived a thunderbolt, an earthquake, or a tsunami. You've seen survivors of an earthquake wandering around looking dazed. You might not lose your bearings or the ability to speak coherently, but it's possible that you will *feel* as if you are walking around in a daze. You might even give yourself a good shake every now and then, take a look in the mirror, and peer deep inside yourself to make sure you're the same person.

   Everything and everyone looks the same, but you are not the same person, and that makes some things in your life seem out of sync. "Time heals all wounds" is one of those sayings that are definitely true, so you *will* regain your equilibrium. The road is bumpy, and there are still a few more stages to go through before you see the light at the end of the tunnel.

2. *Sadness.* This is part of the "What have I done?" stage. It is characterized by disbelief, the sense that perhaps you lost

your marbles. Although your friends and your family might have cheered you on or at least patted you on the back during the first stage, in this stage you don't quite agree with them anymore. You keep checking yourself. You feel as though your heart has been ripped out of your chest.

Even if you liked him only a little bit or the relationship was sort of new, the sadness is poignant. Fleetwood Mac isn't helping anymore, and whenever the phone rings, you are hoping that it's him, and he's ready to say, "Babe, you know that thing you really wanted me to do that I wouldn't? I would so love a second chance to do it. I'll do anything!" It doesn't happen, however. You push out your bottom lip and leave it there for at least a week, maybe two. As long as you try to limit calling yourself names, nothing is wasted time. You have the opportunity to learn from every experience.

3. *Commitment.* Did you really just do it? You pinch yourself and wonder one of several things: why the world didn't explode, why you didn't implode, or why he looked so dumbfounded, unaffected, or amused. You recommit: "Yeah, I said it, and I meant it." Then you make some kind of a physical move to solidify what you have said. You pack the stuff that reminds you of him (or of the two of you together), pull pictures off your bulletin board, throw your cell phone out the window (this is the one you'll regret most quickly), and put the jewelry he gave you back in a box and on your stack of things to get rid of.

   Sometimes you move only the essentials; at other times you go haywire and put everything that ever reminded you of any time you spent together in a big black plastic garbage bag. The overall feeling is one of surprise *and* relief.

You might say to yourself, "It's about time," "I should have done this ages ago," or "What a weight off of me." Maybe you are quivering a little, but it's all interspersed with a bit of pride. You are sticking to your guns.

4. *Rage.* How you went from tearful and pathetic one day to homicidal the next would worry you if you weren't so overcome with vindictive fantasies of how to humiliate him or cause him as much slow, long-lasting bodily pain as possible. Your moods swing back and forth: from hating yourself for staying as long you did (you saw the signs and knew what was going on, and now you feel like a big sucker) to hating him—what a manipulative meathead! He took you for a ride, played with your emotions, then did nothing to keep you from going. In a sense, he tossed you away like a rag.

   You hope that he burns in hell—twice. You lie awake at night thinking about revenge. You consider taking up boxing, jujitsu, or karate—anything that will let you take out your anger in a constructive way. You swear that you will reinvent yourself to make him realize that he made the worst mistake of his life by not doing that simple little thing you asked. You will laugh and saunter off with your new boyfriend, Armando, who loves taking ballroom dancing classes, who spends time with your family, who never snores or hogs the covers, and who thinks Heidi Klum is too skinny.

5. *Resolution.* One day your alarm clock goes off and you get out of bed, remembering that it's casual Friday, so you can wear jeans to work. Your next thought is that it's a good thing you remembered to get milk for your coffee last night, because the old milk has expired. Five, ten, maybe fifteen minutes go by, and all of a sudden it hits you: you haven't

thought of *him.* You check your watch: it's been almost fifteen minutes. You look around. Days, even weeks, have passed since the breakup, but his voice, name, or face was the first thing you thought of when the alarm went off, and now, finally, here is the day you've been waiting for.

The rest of the day or the weekend may not follow as easily, but today marks the beginning of *resolution,* which means that you've moved on. You may revert from time to time when you hear a certain song or run across a note from him, but a good part of you has accepted the reality and moved on. The next few weeks you'll waffle, but the constant fear of running into him will diminish, and the panic of hoping or dreading that it's him every time the phone rings will subside. You'll admit that you really don't want him to die a long, painful death. You have moments where you are somewhat realistic: he had some good traits, some bad; it was a good run, just not a good match. You learned a lot, and it could have been much, much worse. Part of recovery is turning the breakup into a good thing. "Now I'll have to get back to the gym. I'll have to take better care of myself. Actually, I'll do some uncluttering all over. I'll focus on me for once." You've successfully gone from asking yourself if you will ever stop crying to wondering who the new cute guy in accounting is. That's progress.

Relapse Danger

Beware of pitfalls in this process. As in any recovery, getting over someone can include a relapse. Sometimes returning to a relationship that's going nowhere relieves the pain temporarily. Just as you've got one foot out the door, he decides he understands how serious you are. You say, "I'm out." He says, "Okay, okay, I give in!" He cuts his hair and gets a job, he goes into rehab, or he finally tells his friends to shove off because they are getting in the way of his true love. However, this tends to happen more in the movies than in real life, where he's unlikely to sustain his new habits. If you feel yourself wavering, several things may be happening:

1. What we may call the relationship or love part of the brain is overcoming the logical or memories-of-bad-times part of the brain. This isn't hard neurology, but your brain does tend to remember the good times more than the bad regarding love. You've literally forgotten how angry you were, how disappointed or enraged he would make you. (Of course, if you do go back, he'll remind you pretty quickly.)
2. You hate being single (or dating), seeing all your friends paired off, and somehow you talk yourself into the idea that if it's not him, you'll die alone with a few dozen cats. Research says that single happy women lead long lives, so work on feeling positive, and if you do bump into Mr. Right or a Mr. Better, good for you. If not, being single is not the kiss of death, and it gives you many liberties that partnered individuals don't have.
3. Deep down you still hope that he'll change. Remember all the myths and the strange ways that the female brain works in thinking that men aren't changing because women haven't explained themselves well enough or because men are just distracted. Somewhere inside you, there is a tiny part of you that still believes that you just didn't explain it to him with enough enthusiasm, that he really does have a memory problem, or that he just didn't realize how important it was to you. In just a few more weeks or months, he could have gotten it. Our comment on this is that you are

not fed up enough. You believe that he needs one more try? Go for it. Do it until you realize the truth: he won't change, because it's inconvenient, it's not really his personality, or he doesn't really care what you want. Once you truly learn this, you can move on.

Friends, Family, and the Fallout

How do the people in your life react to your decision to walk away from Mr. Almost? Most women we talked to reported variations on "I told you so" from their network of friends and family. Some women reported that there were a few friends who refused to believe that they were really throwing in the towel, after so many false alarms. Others raised an eyebrow or bluntly tsk-tsked about the "wasted time."

Remember, you've vented your frustration about him to your friends so often that you might not get much sympathy. Your best friend tries to conceal the fact that she can't stand him, especially since he's put you through such hell, whereas your mother thinks that you are too picky and wishes you'd lighten up. Regardless, everyone is tired of hearing how frustrating it was to get him to give up chewing tobacco or downloading Internet porn, and they are unlikely to express much interest in hearing you rehash, step by step, each failed attempt to get him to change.

Don't interpret their sighs, eye rolling, or grunts as a lack of interest. They just don't believe that it is really the end, and for good reason. In a few months, when they see you've decided for good, you'll get the response you wanted. You'll get respect for standing your ground, a pat on the back for finally making the move, and a hug for finding yourself and doing what is important to you.

Letting Your Imagination Get the Best of You

One common element of relationships with so-called potential is that they sap a woman's energy. You leave it, six months or six years later, feeling washed out, as if you were twenty years older—weathered, cynical, and jaded. You are truly emotionally exhausted. Some of the fatigue comes from feeling hypervigilant, and some comes from having to repeatedly check yourself and reality because you're starting to feel crazy. You repeat yourself, look for creative ways to express your urgency, and grit your teeth. What exactly is running through your head? Some things are pure fantasy, and some—very unlikely, however—are real. The keyword here is *unlikely*.

- *Your biggest fantasy*. He finally comes to the conclusion that he will lose you once and for all if he does not change. He then wholeheartedly does what you've asked, without resentment. He runs out into traffic after your cab as you leave for the airport, waving evidence of his self-revision. (A paycheck? A puppy? An engagement ring?) You stop the cab, run to him, and make out like teenagers in the middle of Fifth Avenue—at Christmas time. Then it starts to snow. Sigh.

  Reality check: He makes a temporary change in order to get you back. He goes on a few job interviews; then you find a woman's phone number in his pocket, which he swears he was holding for a friend; and he uses lots of lines like "Baby, I'm trying." Then you see him slipping back into his old self and remember why you broke up with him in the first place. This may take as little as five to ten minutes.

- *Your big fear*. Less than twenty-four hours after the breakup, you are on your second box of tissues and your third pint of ice cream, and you're still wearing the pajamas that you put on yesterday. You haven't looked in a mirror in a day or more. You drag yourself to the computer to check for supportive e-mails from friends. Then you find yourself on his Facebook page, where there is a picture of your all-too-recent ex partying the very night of your breakup. He looks so handsome and fun. Some woman is with him in the picture, and she's also on his new friends list, thanking him for the great evening.

Reality check: First of all, you broke up with him because he's a jerk, had his head in the clouds, and was a lazy two-faced whatever. Now that he's behaving that way again, you should not be surprised. It's messed up that he would flaunt his newfound freedom in a forum that he knows you can view, but that's his problem. Get off the computer and get into the shower. Use this as more proof that this is not the guy you want to be with in life. The bottom line is that you broke up with him, and he is having a great time. Actually, not only is he having a good time, he is letting everyone know that he is having a great time. Call your friends who will tell you the cold hard truth and not the lie you want to hear.

- *Your even bigger fear*. This could possibly be your *biggest* fear: you leave him, he changes, and then someone else gets this great reformed guy.

  Reality check: Whoever gets him next may have to go through all the grueling steps to find out that he is a pathological liar or a guy who listens to heavy-metal music exclusively (regardless of what her likes are). She might, however, just happen to love that kind of music and also be a pathological liar herself, but she might hate his sister, his dog, or his love of the outdoors. She might be clueless about his drawbacks and not be annoyed by anything because she grew up with six brothers and she's just happy when he remembers to put the toilet seat back down. Regardless, your main point is to remember that you two don't make a good couple.

You aren't a bad person for hating the fact that he "recycles" his gym clothes, and he isn't a bad guy for thinking that he is somehow being ecologically responsible by wearing the same musty, sweat-stained shorts every day for a week.

What to Do

It's so easy after a breakup to find yourself at loose ends. Sunday used to be the day that you would get the newspaper and go to the park together. You used to barbecue on Friday afternoon. Wednesday was taco night. Now you have all that time to yourself, and you just don't know what to do with it. Here are a few suggestions:

- Treat yourself as if you have the flu. Eat well, get lots of rest, and drink a gallon of water. Lie on the couch with a blanket and the shades pulled down. Take a break from e-mail and the telephone.
- Be kind to yourself. Think about what you'd do for your best friend if she had just broken up with her boyfriend. Would you take her to a spa? Treat her to lunch? Show up at her place with ice cream and a movie? Do these things for yourself instead.
- Address your mental health. Are you depressed? Classic signs of depression include a loss of interest in daily activities, hopelessness, crying spells, trouble sleeping, too much sleeping, weight gain, or weight loss. If any of these sound familiar, consider going to talk to a therapist. Just remember that it's normal for you to be grieving now; your depression is the natural result of the circumstances in your life, not a genetic chemical imbalance to be treated with medication.
- Start to find yourself again. Who were you before you were in a relationship? What did you let go of to make room for that

man? Who do you want to be? Have you been talking about taking a pottery class for five years? Now is the time to do it.

- If your friends force you to go out, be realistic. You might not stay out dancing till dawn with a handsome stranger on your very first trip back to the club. You might break down crying at the bar. Don't make a habit of it, but if you become weepy for a while, that's appropriate.
- Do only fun things. See a wacky comedy movie (not a depressing drama). Go ice skating and drink hot cocoa.
- Keep moving. Make a list of things you want to get done in the day, and then do them. If you don't, tell yourself that that's okay, too.
- Unclutter your home. You know that you've been meaning to reorganize your CD collection, your filing system, or your computer, and you never had the time. Now you do!
- Therapize, whether it's writing in a journal, reading self-help books, or seeing a therapist. Extreme times bring all sorts of personal issues to the surface, such as loss and trust. Take the time and care to deal with whatever troubles you.
- Do things that make you feel good immediately, whether it's a massage, shopping, or calling your best friend.
- Preen! If people are telling you that you look good, it will make you feel better. Ultimately, it will help you to meet someone new (and better than your ex).
- Validate the feelings of loss that you are rightfully experiencing. Breaking up is hard, and this kind of breakup is the worst. You are right to mourn for your relationship.
- Get through one day at time. If you keep picking up the phone to call him, just focus on not calling him for that day.

Don't think about the whole week or the rest of your life. Focus on just that one day.

Relapse Reminders

One lonely, rainy night you call him. He comes over, one thing leads to the next obvious thing, and you fall off the wagon. Maybe a day or two goes by and then *wham*! You get a reminder of why you left. He gets a phone call at three o'clock in the morning—which he takes, in the bathroom. After he has promised you that he is sober, you find gin under the sink. He said those losers you hate are not even his friends, but then you find them on his couch. Nothing has changed. Don't beat yourself up. You just needed a refresher. Thank the universe, or whatever deity you pray to, for reminding you why you're better off without this guy. Your hope was sweet, but the reminder was a slap in the face. Take your medicine with pride and get back on your regimen of healing and moving forward.

> "It was as if I went into autopilot," Yoshi, a student at the University of Pennsylvania, told us. "Once I even called his family's home in Virginia and hung up a few times. I was so mortified. I knew I had to do something about it. I had done such a great job in the beginning, making him think that I didn't care that we broke up, that I had moved on and was unaffected. When I woke up the next day and realized that I had called, I cried and just wanted to die. I was so embarrassed and angry at myself."

We know that alcohol lessens inhibitions, but at least you used to have to find a phone book and a quarter before you could embarrass yourself. Today, mobile phones with electronic phone books and e-mail sit innocently on the bar as you down a couple of drinks. There is practically no barrier between you and him, and it would be so easy to just reach out and tell him what you really think of him.

Drinking and dialing happens because you feel that you have unfinished business with the person you are calling, the victim of your drunken wrath. These calls fall into two categories: the "I still love you" call and the "Let me tell you how much I hate you" call. There is some overlap here. You may call him intending to deliver one sort of message but end up delivering the other. What they both have in common is embarrassment and unease the next day.

As soon as the alarm rang, Samantha felt a huge sense of regret. Something bad had happened, something very bad, although she couldn't pinpoint what, possibly because of the distracting, pounding headache or the dryness in her mouth. Her eyes wandered around the room, then came to a slow, fuzzy focus on the phone. The phone! There it was, in the middle of the room, next to the heels she had thrown off when she came home last night after a few too many. She cringed, knowing that she had come home and dialed her ex again.

Now she just had to figure out if she had spoken to him or his machine and try to piece together the conversation. The last time Samantha had called, she woke him up, screamed at him, cried, and then finished by asking him to come back. What had happened this time? Oh, how she wished she had drunk less or had hidden the phone before going out! She put on Radiohead, pulled the covers over her head, and wanted to die of shame.

How to Handle Drink-and-Dial Syndrome

- Recognize that you have unfinished business and that these calls are proof that you still have emotional wounds that need to be healed. When you've been sober, you have managed to convince yourself that you are doing pretty well. The drunken evidence shows otherwise.

- Take some precautions until you have a grip on your issues. A sticky note on the phone that reads "You will want to die if you call him again" could help. If you're at a bar with your cell phone, you can hand it over to your friends after your second drink. Try reentering your ex's name in your phone so that if you dial it, the screen will flash "Hang up now, before you regret it!"
- When you are drunk and feeling vulnerable, write a letter to him. Really get it all out. Be maudlin. Stain the paper with your tears. Remember, this is a healing exercise, not correspondence. Whatever happens, *do not send this letter*! Burn it.
- Take up a sport or another activity that will help you to release the pain you are feeling. This could be boxing or therapy; either is better than drunk-dialing and the subsequent embarrassment. Find a more appropriate outlet for your outbreak.

What-Ifs and Doubts

It's impossible to avoid second-guessing yourself, which should, in a way, make you feel better. If you've already been running through a litany of self-doubt, feel comfort in knowing that nearly everyone looks back at past relationships with questions. You will wonder, "What if I had tried harder? What if I had been more patient? After all, there are reasons he is the way he is. Maybe his past scarred him, maybe he has trust issues because of his last relationship, or maybe he was lonely as a child and never learned the skills for interacting well with others."

Maybe you're going to win the lottery, move to Monte Carlo, and marry Leonardo DiCaprio, but we don't recommend counting on it. You've arrived at this point only through trying your very, very best to make this work. You would never have broken up with him if you still thought you had a decent shot at persuading him to meet you in the middle.

If you find yourself making a million excuses for his behavior, consider that maybe part of you feels sorry for him. Even though he's disappointed you, exaggerated, lied, and manipulated you, part of you just knows that it must be because of some childhood trauma. How could he be honest and vulnerable after his mother was so mean to him? How could he be comfortable with intimacy after his father left when he was so young?

The flip side of this is the implication that your life has been so rosy by comparison that you can handle huge relationship responsibilities. This line of thinking may make you wonder if you should meet him more than halfway. He may not be able to be completely honest because of his messed-up family, but you have to be truthful. Was *your* childhood perfect? Are you a relationship superhero? You are honest because it's important to you, not because you have a great relationship with your father. You are thoughtful because you care about your boyfriend, not because you had a house on a lake when you were a child.

Even if you aren't rethinking the breakup because you feel bad for him, you might still sympathize with him. He has screwed up all his relationships and will probably end up alone (unlike you). Just remember that feeling bad for him, whether or not it involves your making excuses for his behavior, makes you feel superior. You pity him; now imagine how you would feel if you overheard him saying that he pities you. It's pretty yucky, isn't it? In some way, it makes you feel better, bigger, and more powerful to look down on him in this seemingly benevolent fashion. Keep this in mind.

Musicians to listen to: Amy Winehouse, Fleetwood Mac

Musicians not to listen to: Elliot Smith, Death Cab for Cutie

Movies to see: *Swingers, Eternal Sunshine of the Spotless Mind*

A Repeat or a Polar Opposite?

It was the last straw. You've broken up. You just couldn't stand it anymore. You found another woman's phone number, saw him smoking inside the house, watched him come through the door two hours late, and found poker chips in his pants. You pack and you are out. Maybe you go back to your little black book right away, or maybe your girlfriends take you out to a bar to drown your sorrows in a margarita (or four). You glance across the bar. Do you stop to stare at the guy who looks like your ex's brother, or do you find yourself attracted to the guy who resembles him the least?

The "Kicking Him to the Curb" Myth

Once upon a time there was a woman, someone in a faraway part of the country, who kicked her man to the curb. He drank from the milk carton one time too many. She caught him, red-handed, standing in front of the open refrigerator with his head tilted back, glug-glug-glugging from the container. This time she wasn't accepting that he was finishing the milk in the carton. This time she wasn't believing that he simply couldn't find a glass. She snapped. She hauled him by the back of his belt to the sidewalk and kicked him to the curb. Later she put his things outside the door, and, rumor has it, he is still drinking from a milk carton—across town at his new girlfriend's house.

Thus the "kicking him to the curb" myth was born: the notion that the relationship ended in an instant, liberating moment. Kicking him to the curb is actually the end of a process, however.

Talk-show audiences yell to the tearful girlfriend as if all she has to do is pull a switch. Kicking him to the curb is usually a slow, painful process that ranges from disappointment to anger to rage to sadness to a slight glimmer of hope, going around and around until you break up.

Then you get back together for some not-so-magical reason. You do it all again, until finally you come to the realization that this is who he is and who he will be until the day he dies.

As we said earlier, one of the reasons for taking him back is the fear that all girlfriends who look for potential have: that he'll change after they've left. The next woman will get the new and improved version of him. They did all this work, just for her to saunter up and wonder why a great guy like him is single.

It's not actually like that, however. The woman who gets him next has no inkling of what you had to do just to get him to where he is. That can be really infuriating to you. How many times have women said, "I was with him when he was really messed up. I cleaned up after him, and she reaps the rewards!" In a way that may be true, but deep down he is still the same man who has mommy issues or a sarcastic sense of humor that no one likes. So what really happens after he picks himself up from the curb and saunters to the other side of town? Here are two sample scenarios:

1. The mommy issues don't really bother *her.* Perhaps she has lower or different expectations than you do. In chapter 1, we talked about Prince Charming potential (PCP) and how every woman has a different set of attributes for the man of her dreams. For example, let's say you couldn't stand that your guy worked on a reality television show six months of the year, so you convinced him to take a job that would keep him away only a month, at the most. Nevertheless, you still missed him and wanted him to be around more, but he wouldn't agree to another job. You finally broke it off. The next woman he

seeks might be less stressed about the job and more concerned about dating a man who doesn't cheat on her. His PCP, in terms of her priorities, is different from what it was for you. Instead of her getting the transformed man you think she's getting, she has a whole other mess of bones to pick.

2. You nursed him through his dark days, brought him to his first AA meeting, and told him that you were leaving him so that he could work on his sobriety. You had to—for both your sakes. Even after you split up, however, you took his phone calls, arranged to pick up his mail, and gave him a shoulder to lean on when he was down and out. One year of sobriety passes, and he calls you to tell you that he's met someone and is in love. You want to reach through the phone and throttle him. You have been with him every step of the way, and now he is clean and sober and with *her*?

The soul searching that this creates can be extremely painful, but not necessarily shocking. Many times, the transformed man needs a fresh start with someone who hasn't seen him at his worst, such as when he was sobbing after a night of hard partying or the time he spent all of his money on booze and you had to lend him cash for his rent. He might not admit it to you, but the memories that are associated with that time bring up feelings of humiliation beyond your wildest dreams. So now that he has a new lease on life, he has a new girlfriend.

As much as this hurts, this is one of those times that the adage "It wasn't meant to be" rings true. Did you really want to spend the rest of your life preparing yourself for the day that he decides he can have just one drink? Would you really want to be with someone who will probably end up trading one addiction for another?

The Bottom Line

Whether his issue was alcohol, mean-spiritedness, or just talking with his mouth full, the woman who ends up with him won't be rejoicing in the streets over her new and improved perfect specimen. She will end up with her own list of things that didn't bother her at first but are now eating her up inside. What about all the work you did? You can pretty much bet your bottom dollar that sooner or later there will be cracks in the surface and that she will have to repair them or else kick him to the curb, just as you did.

Feeling Like an Idiot

Every woman who has had a project boyfriend reaches this stage. It's not typical of other breakups, but since you've been trying to convince yourself and others that this will succeed, this stage is extra hard. You feel like such a heel.

Part of what makes it so confusing is how difficult it is to remember how ugly the last fight became. It's kind of fuzzy now, and you wonder if it really was that bad—bad enough to give up hope on him?

Each time the fight or argument becomes more heated or frustrating, the bar for what you will tolerate goes up. All of a sudden you are putting up with him repeatedly breaking his promises, because you're used to it. How did your last argument go from "never again" to the tenth or fifteenth time of "one more chance"?

Don't forget what we stressed before. Part of the dynamic is that your brain is set up to forget the bad and remember the good. This serves a biological function: to get the two of you back together and, according to natural selection, to procreate.

The Point

Understanding why you picked a project boyfriend and how you participated in the scenario that played out is important. How did your myths, your fantasies, your projections, and your expectations influence you to stay for as long as you did? How did they enable you to continue to believe that he could change, despite the fact that he didn't?

Understanding this in detail is important so that the next man you choose isn't the same, so that you don't repeat your mistakes in some weird way of wanting to make it all right. "I couldn't change the last one, so, doggone it, I'll really do it with this one." It's also important so you don't go in the completely opposite direction because you've been so scalded by your last project.

Being able to see the next guy's strengths and weaknesses and what he really could and would change for you is important. Maybe you'll find one who is perfect—who won't bite his nails, who always puts his dishes in the sink, who is outgoing enough but not flirty, who is motivated but not a workaholic. If you don't, however, we hope that by now you can recognize when he has no intention of changing that trait and when your diamond-in-the-rough guy really does have potential.

10

One for the Boys

With all this focus on you and your thoughts, we thought we'd try to look at this briefly from his perspective. Here goes.

What was he thinking? What *is* he thinking? *Is* he thinking?

You'd like to think that you can read his mind by watching for the creases around his eyes when he smiles, by the way he blinks and moves his lips, and by his body language and posture. You are smart enough to know, however, that although you wish he were looking back at you and thinking, "Damn, how did I get this lucky?", he is actually trying to figure out if you will finish making brunch before the game starts.

"Sara would ask me how I remembered our meeting, and she loved hearing the details. It was like a little kid's bedtime story for her. She loved sort of reliving that first meeting and the beginning of our relationship. She wanted to know what I was thinking, play by play. It was funny to me that while I was looking at the whole picture and thinking, 'Wow, she's cute,' she was scrutinizing me from top to bottom and analyzing every word the entire evening. She remembers everything. It's almost scary."

It's the same with the negotiations and the power struggle that are part of trying to meet each other's needs. You hope and pray that he has no problem accommodating your pet peeves or, if this is hard, that he sees the prize (you) as being worth it. Unfortunately, you are often left looking at the man you thought you knew so well and wondering why there is a discrepancy between what he is saying and what he is doing or what he is doing and what he should be doing, according to you. To be fair, though, there is a "his side of the story" in this.

Women are constantly evaluating—whom should they date, and should they continue to date these men? Deadlines, whether self-imposed or biological, create pressure for women to choose quickly and wisely. Add to this the sad notion that a relationship that is long is successful, but a short one is not. A long relationship without wedding vows is a "waste of time." This makes a very small window for success in relationships, but it doesn't have to be that way.

Your friends and family make the stress worse by emphasizing the importance of "settling down"; then there is your own desire to have a long-term partner. The pressure of women being valued for a shorter amount of time due to sexism and ageism also makes women feel rushed.

Men seem to articulate the situation very well. "At age thirty-five," says Jason, "every woman I date is looking for a husband. I can feel it from across the room. I know they are trying to be laid back and carefree, but most are flipping out because their friends are married, their sisters are married, and their parents want them to be. Sometimes they can be cool for a while, then the 'where is this going' questions start. It's predictable."

In talking with and polling men, we found that they often had mixed feelings about being coupled. One seemingly dyed-in-the-wool bachelor said, "It's true, I am holding out in changing because I don't know if I want to be totally compatible and give her the impression that the next step is a long-term relationship or marriage. I look at my married friends, and they aren't so happy, so why am I supposed to be striving to be like them?"

Marriage is viewed by numerous men today as the kiss of death, whereas many women can't see past their fantasy wedding day. Men seem to be more cognizant of the problems that come after the wedding, and research supports them (see Bella DePaulo's *Singled Out: How Singles Are Stereotyped, Stigmatized, and Ignored, and Still Live Happily Ever After*). The people who report being the happiest are those who are most satisfied with their household finances, and the next are those who have good health. Being married comes in third.

She's Got Potential?

What happens when the shoe is on the other foot? In general, men don't try to fix their partners in the same way that women do; however, there are some men who will date a woman and try to change her. Three scenarios are detailed below:

1. Pretty Woman syndrome: A man meets a woman, sees her as down-and-out or as a "damsel in distress," and saves her by helping her to straighten out.

2. I-Know-What-Is-Best-for-You syndrome: My opinion of what you need trumps your opinion of what you want, because I know what is better for you. Period.
3. Perfect Partner syndrome: A man wants a woman who can be his "mini-me." They should be interlocking puzzle pieces, a round peg and a round hole, or twin flames.

As you go about eliciting changes in your man, he is probably thinking something like "If she's so intent on changing me, then she should change a few things herself. Why should I be the only one expected to make transformations?" A man who feels himself becoming a project boyfriend may not enjoy being forced to change his tune—or his grooming habits. You can almost hear the guy saying, "I'm not changing for anyone! Take me as I am or not at all." Thus, in order to keep him, it may be necessary to compromise: "If you work on quitting smoking, I'll stop biting my nails."

Coming to such an agreement not only takes some of the focus off him but also puts you on the same team. Instead of there being one person railing against another, both people are working together to become better people. Some of the best, most successful relationships are between two people who bring out the best in each other.

Real Stories

"Kathy's family was crazy. She'd spend days at my house, and I'd feel bad about her going back to hers. Finally I married her to get her out of there. It was way too early for me, but I felt guilty about leaving her there."

"Cheryl was a workaholic and obsessive about details, I knew this was bad for her in the long run, but she didn't. I keep thinking that if I can break her of this crazy routine, she will be able to relax with me."

"Patricia was lazy. She loved napping, and her idea of the perfect weekend involved the couch and movies. If she loved me, she'd at least try her hand at sports and get some exercise."

"Kari was always the social butterfly. She was the wild one. She was the organizer. I wanted her to pay attention to me—only me. I wanted to own her. Her erratic attention was addictive. I wanted to take her home and be able to spend time together—without alcohol, without an audience, just her and me. Although she would do that every once in a while, she'd soon get antsy. 'This is who I am, this is how I was when you met me, so why are you trying to get me to stay still?' It was so frustrating. I loved that she was popular and wanted to change the world and do more and more, but didn't she see what a catch I was? None of the people around her cared about her the way I did. I just had to make her see that."

Sex: When He Wants to Change the Way You Do It

> If we treat people as they are, we make them worse. If we treat people as they ought to be, we help them become what they are capable of becoming.
>
> –Goethe

There's no doubt about it, sex can make or break a relationship. Even two people who are extremely compatible in every other way get in the sack and stumble all over each other. Some who spit venom at each other during the day rip their clothes off in lust-fueled passion at night. It's mostly chemistry. Smells, sights, sounds, and sensation all work in symbiosis to make it good or, unfortunately, gross.

What happens if your man complains that you don't perform oral sex, that you never initiate, or that you turn him down too often? Maybe you like it on top and he likes it from behind—and lately, it's turned into a source of contention. He calls you selfish, and you think he's degrading you.

Maybe you've made it farther than most, way past the three-year itch that has become the norm these days, and sex has become rote, boring, and mechanical.

"I'm a guy. Sex is the most important thing to me. In the beginning, we did it so often, we just decided it was better to take our meals in bed than eat at the table. Now, we have sex twice a week, and I'm not happy about it. Jackie better step up to the plate or I'm gonna start looking in other places for what I need."

Change Her Back

The number one complaint guys have is that their girlfriends have changed. When they met, these men will say, the women were fun and carefree, "party girls," and then as time passed they started nagging and not taking care of themselves. If you then talk to the women, you find that they wonder how they are supposed to keep up that level of partying and grooming.

"Sure I was dressed up and all sexy when I met him, but I never said that I was going to wear stilettos when I cleaned the house. I wanted him to love me for my heart, my personality. He seemed to feel that I had put out a false impression of who I was. It was the same with sex: we had tons of hot sex when we met, but then when we were spending more time together, there were mornings we had to get up for work, so thrashing around all night was something I couldn't do. I couldn't, and didn't want to, be up all night in contortions. He kept pouting and telling me he missed 'that girl.'"

Across the board the complaint is the same. "She used to be skinny. Now she eats all the time and is getting fat." "She was so outgoing, and now she never wants to go to parties." "She was always so cool and laid back. Now she's always on my case." Guys feel duped—as if the woman they met was just a facade of her real self. If you've learned anything from reading this book, you will know that people aren't in the habit of misrepresenting themselves, per se. They are just trying to make a good first impression. More than likely there are a few reasons for your "change":

1. You're in love. Duh! You would much rather stay in and snuggle with your beau than hit a bar, down some shots, and come home smelling like an ashtray.
2. What's the point? Your motive for trolling the clubs looking so dolled up was to get attention from a guy like him.
3. It takes a lot of time and effort to dress to impress every day. Now that you're more comfortable in your relationship, you don't feel the pressure to glam it up.
4. You're nesting, and that means staying in, cooking dinner, and spending time alone together.
5. Maybe you *were* putting on a front just until he fell head over heels for you.

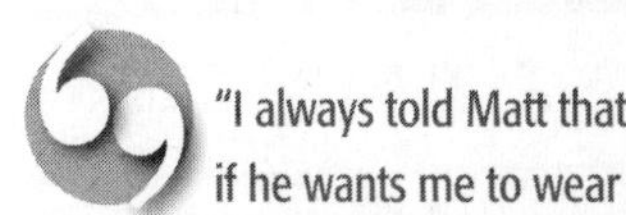

"I always told Matt that if he wants me to wear heels, then he should buy me a pair. I think it's sexy when a guy buys me shoes, and I'm much more likely to wear them if he gives them to me."

For men who miss the woman they met, changing her back is not as hard as it seems. Women change their minds as often as they change their hairstyles, so it goes without saying that they'll change their minds again in due time. It's much easier to coach people back to what they were than to make them into something new. This presents an opportunity to expedite the natural progression in an effective way.

Other Changes He's Griping About

- She has become frumpy.
- She has gained weight.
- She doesn't show interest in my job.
- She has lost the drive to accomplish that I found so sexy.
- She is obsessed with details and errands and has become a nag; she worries.

"When Joe and I first got together, I always jumped at the opportunity to go out with him, no matter where he wanted to go or what he wanted to do. I was so smitten, he could have taken me to McDonald's and I would have been happy. When I realized that he wasn't going anywhere, I spoke up more often about what we did. I could tell he was shocked and that he wondered where the quiet, obliging girl had gone."

- She talks about nothing but the kids.
- She no longer treats me as sexy.
- She is not novel or interesting anymore.
- She worries about money and becomes upset about my spending.
- She is jealous of my friends and my past.

Maybe the things that bothered him before somehow bother him more now, or they become more evident later. Perhaps, for example, you were never one to watch sports, and in the beginning the attraction was so fierce that it didn't seem to matter all that much to him. As time passed and baseball season commenced, however, the fact that you opted to watch *Wall-E* over the St. Louis Cardinals game started to make him uneasy. Now every time a game is on, he complains that you never want to watch a game anymore.

Maybe you always acted a little crazy after a few drinks. In fact, the night you met, you were playing air guitar after your third drink. Now he rolls his eyes every time you order another gin and tonic. Like an itch that won't go away, the issues that once felt small can grow to be the size of an elephant.

The Myth of the "Perfect" Woman

Perfect is a word that should never be used in relationships. People grow up in different homes, with different types of parents as role models. What's perfect for one person spells disaster for another, just like the saying "One man's trash is another man's treasure." Although compatibility is a possibility to strive for, perfection is not. In the end, the most important part of a relationship is that the partners share the same interests, the same goals about family (number of children to have, to live in the city or country), and similar ideals.

> "I'm hesitant to commit because I don't want to find myself settling. Unlike my friends, I want to be married only once. So I am going to hold out for the perfect girl—the one who likes me exactly the way I am."

As in the 1985 movie *Weird Science*, it's a common fantasy of men to want to create their idea of the "perfect" woman. Give her a body like actress and model Kelly LeBrock, the IQ of Albert Einstein, and the cool factor of Aerosmith's Steven Tyler, and presto—she is the real version of a blow-up doll. However, real women are just like real men: chock full of problems and possessing some potential, a lot of potential, or none at all.

Men who assume that they will one day meet the woman of their dreams will be disappointed when they find out that she tends to be a little stinky after a long workout, that she cries when

A Sign of the Times?

A study published in February 2009 by University of Iowa sociologists Christine Whelan and Christine Boxer has been conducted every decade since 1939 in order to find out the characteristics that are most desirable in men and women and their order of importance. In 1939, chastity was more important than intelligence and financial status. Nowadays, dependability, emotional stability, and intelligence are topping the list of what both sexes want in a mate. Could it be that men and women are finally seeing eye to eye?

her boss gives her negative feedback, and that she rarely puts her fork to her mouth without spilling food on her shirt. The male fantasy continues to exist, however. Because men are driven by sex (and the biological need to procreate), it shouldn't come as a shock to anyone to report that first and foremost, a man wants a good-looking woman by his side. The fantasy of this half woman, half robot is perpetuated in the media, in the movies, and pretty much everywhere else you look.

Three Qualities That Make Her "Perfect"

1. *Looks.* Every culture has its own version of what is considered beautiful, and a man wants a beautiful woman by his side. Many men also want eternal youth—for the woman, that is. These men get older, but the women they date are always the same age.
2. *Domesticity.* Ah, the old "woman belongs in the kitchen" stereotype. Women have come a long way since June Cleaver (thank God for delivery menus and nannies), but there is still a steadfast conviction that women should take care of the house, fold the clothes, and make dinner for the family.
3. *Adoration.* Say what you will about sexual equality. When all is said and done, men want to feel respected and looked up to.

Real Stories

"To me, Deirdre's wanting to change the way I dressed was just her being controlling. Whenever the topic came up, I'd feel myself get really angry. It felt as if she was talking down to me, judging me and wanting to control my actions."

"After my mom had my brother, she became really anxious, and only later did I realize that it was postpartum depression. She had to clean everything and know where everything was, and if it was out of place she had a meltdown. My dad was either called to help or blamed. I remember thinking that no woman would ever tell me what to do. It didn't matter how much I loved her or she loved me, I couldn't tolerate that situation again."

"Every time Lisa would hint at something she wanted me to do, I could feel myself tense up. I'd be passive-aggressive and 'forget' for as long as possible, then finally do it halfway. I hoped that this would discourage her from asking for anything else, but it didn't."

"Tara was relentless. She'd ask me every fifteen seconds if I had done what she wanted. I never did it because I wanted to, but only because I wanted her to shut up."

Partnership as a Process

Maybe at this point you realize that your man has so much more potential than you ever thought, or maybe you've come to the conclusion that you've taken a detail and made it much bigger—he really has much less potential than you originally thought. Regardless, the main point is that rather than feeling as if you are waiting for him to see the light, you now have more choices about how you think. Rather than aiming for perfection, you can see that partnership is a *process* in which you can make active choices rather than just hope for things to go your way. Mostly, you are now less a victim of your good intentions to fix him. You understand that you are so stubborn in hanging in there because you see a glimmer of hope for a great partner in him.

Have you decided to leave him? If so, we hope that it's with less sadness and regret and with the understanding that it's not a failure in your project. In fact, the decision you made may be one that is protective of yourself, and maybe you can see how the relationship helped you to grow as well.

Are you thinking of staying, at least for a while? If so, we hope that you have a plan not to sweat the small things and to put your foot down about others.

Love is so much more complicated than just walking off into the sunset. *Really* understanding your motives, questioning your goals, and accurately assessing if he does have potential (and not just wishing that he does) can lead to your finding love.

Index